Earth Moves

Writing **Architecture**

A project of the Anyone Corporation

The MIT Press Cambridge, Massachusetts London, England

Earth Moves

The Furnishing of Territories

Bernard Cache translated by Anne Boyman

edited by Michael Speaks

© 1995 Massachusetts Institute of Technology

This book was printed and bound in the United States of America.

Library of Congress Cataloging-in-Publication Data

Cache, Bernard.
[Terre meuble. English]
Earth moves : the furnishing of territories / Bernard Cache ; translated by Anne Boyman ; edited by Michael Speaks.
p. cm. — (Writing architecture)
Translation of an unpublished French manuscript written in 1983 under the title: Terre meuble.
Includes bibliographical references.
ISBN-10: 0-262-53130-5 (pbk. : alk. paper)
ISBN-13: 978-0-262-53130-6 (pbk. : alk. paper)
1. Space (Architecture) 2. Architecture—Philosophy. 3. Form (Aesthetics) I. Speaks, Michael. II. Title. III. Series.
NA2765.C2813 1995
720´.1—dc20   95-17087
                                                      CIP

10   9   8   7   6   5

For Gilles Deleuze

It is in this English-language edition that *Earth Moves* is published for the first time. Written in 1983 under the title *Terre Meuble*, the manuscript might have gone unnoticed had it not been for Gilles Deleuze, who told of its existence in notes to two of his own books. A complex relation attaches Bernard Cache's work to Deleuze's philosophy: Cache followed Deleuze's seminar at the University of Paris for many years, finding in Deleuze a major philosophical inspiration for his own work. Deleuze in turn recognized the originality of Cache, who took up concepts like image, frame, and territory and made them live and move in new ways.

For Deleuze there is a certain foreignness in the force of a conceptual creation, as though what is new is always expressed in a language as yet unspoken and never fully understood. This is certainly true of this book, which takes us off into a strange uncharted conceptual territory in which old words come to be used in new ways and new words are invented in an effort to open out new domains of thought, or to introduce variations in old ones. *Earth Moves* thus offers an unfamiliar picture of architecture itself, speaking something of a strange new tongue in architectural discourse. It therefore proposes not only an original view of architecture, but also an original way of doing architectural theory.

What, then, is the shift in ground by which the concepts of image, frame, and territory start to move in these new ways? In the first instance, one might speak of a basic shift from the problematic of representation, central to the pictorial arts since the last century, to a problematic of space and movement. What Cache calls "images" are analyzed in terms of framing and territories rather than in terms of model and imitation, figuration and abstraction. In this shift, architecture acquires a singular new role, quite different from the traditional notion of a closed system or architectonic; and a new question arises: how to show or create the kind of movement that is prior to the representation of stable objects, and so introduce a new dynamic conception of both image and architecture.

Cache calls his book a "classifier of images." But what is an image? What does it mean to understand image in terms of a space that is prior to representation? An image is not a picture. It is not a representation or an imitation of an external object, and we must therefore get away from the Platonic view that connects seeing to essential forms, as well as from the Cartesian variant on this view in which an image is conceived as an internal or mental picture of an external object. Cache envisages instead a universe where objects are not stable but may undergo variations, giving rise to new possibilities of seeing. He works with the Bergsonian idea of image that Deleuze develops in his study of film: as with the "movement images" and "time images" Deleuze analyzes, we see things as functions of actions in and reactions to a milieu. But since such reactions are not automatic or deterministic and include "zones of indetermination" from which unexpected movement might come, images involve what transpires in the intervals or disparities between things. They are connected through a logic where the whole is not given but always open to variation, as new things are added or new relations made, creating new continuities out of such intervals or disparities. In the unstable dynamic world in which they figure, images are therefore no longer defined by fixed divisions between inside and outside. Rather this division itself comes to shift or move as outside forces cause internal variations or as internal variations create new connections with the outside. In this way we see that images belong to a dynamic rather than a static geography.

Thus for Cache, images, even when they are man-made or artificial, even when they are literally "constructed," always include an element that exceeds the intentions and functions of such making, and links the image to an environment or milieu that is "before man." It follows that there is no environment that can be completely controlled, for there is always new movement that can be released into or out of it. That is what Cache means when he says that inflection is a *primary* sort of image. In every environment there exists the possibility of unpredictable variation, and therefore of inflection images that neither produce the presumed unity or identity of a place nor obey the rule of an abstract Cartesian space, divisible *partes ex partibus*.

The inflection image is thus the kind that is most original or "foreign" in Cache's classification. And it is this kind to which Deleuze alludes when he declares that *Earth Moves* "is essential to any theory of the fold." In the passages of his book *The Fold: Leibniz and the Baroque* devoted to Cache's conception of inflection, Deleuze focuses on his distinction between intrinsic and extrinsic singularity. Extrinsic singularity refers to extrema in a delimited or coordinate space, whereas intrinsic singularity involves an unlimited space, "prior to coordinates, without up or down, right or left, regression or progression." The inflection point is thus a fold point, something like the "elastic points" in Klee in contrast to the hard angles and edges in Kandinsky. It belongs to a topography where a line is not what goes between two points, but a point is the intersection of many lines. Thus it involves a flexible kind of continuity that is not totalized, finalized, or closed. For inflection, while it is first or primary, is also virtual, ungraspable, and fleeting; it is "the pure event of the line or point." The Earth itself thus no longer appears as the immovable, gravitational ground that defines the coordinates or vectors of up/down movement. Rather it spreads out in modulation or variation of its surface such that it is no longer possible to distinguish earth and sky, for the Earth itself has become weightless.

It follows that the concept of the sort of territory in which architecture occurs must itself be altered. A territory is not the immobile closed space of "the context" to which a building must be mimetically adjusted; and the relation of architecture to territory is not that of a complete plan or organized system. Rather architecture is "the art of the frame," and the "architectural" in things is how they are framed. And it is this idea of frame that supplies the second of Cache's concepts to which Deleuze explicitly refers.

In *Qu'est-ce que la philosophie?*, Deleuze and Félix Guattari use the notion of frame to offer another image of what holds up or holds together a work than that of a closed system that internalizes what it preserves. When Cache says that "framing" is an architectural idea before it is a pictorial one, one can thus take him as introducing another idea of frame, that of the enclosing border of a picture, or limit. For framing always involves, at least potentially, the possibility of what Deleuze calls a deframing (*décadrage*), where what is internal to the frame discovers a relation to what is external to it in such a way as to open it up to the outside.

When Cache speaks of "frame images" in architecture, he is thus not referring to the physical frame or skeleton of buildings, and, on the contrary, is attracted to the possibilities of Francis Bacon's images of flesh without bones. Again, one might refer to the concept of "frame" that Deleuze develops in his theory of film: the delimitation from a larger indeterminacy of those elements of which a film is the composition, and which constitute a series of "off" spaces. Indeed, just as one might speak of the "architecture" of films in terms of such framing and deframing of space, there is an almost cinematic quality to Cache's account of the images of territory and architecture, leading to the larger kinds of connection to the new electronic civilization that he says it is our task today to analyze.

In drawing attention to the importance of *Earth Moves*, Deleuze thus stresses the originality of two new concepts: the concept of inflection and the concept of frame. The two concepts describe the new way of thinking, the new "space" Cache is trying to introduce into architecture and architectural discourse. Together they draw a diagram of an unlimited deframable space of possible inflection prior to the delimited space of fixed objects and images. It is a space where new complicating movement is always arising: the space in which the Earth moves. For what the potential of inflection and deframing in our images means is this: that the Earth must move, and that the movements of the Earth are none other than the release of this movement prior to representation and determinate wholes, to fixed coordinates or gravitational vectors. In the words of Paul Klee: "In the universe, movement is given prior to everything."

Anne Boyman

What form or forms will a new architecture take? One answer to this vexing yet crucial question, and indeed one form of the question itself, can be found in the *Architectural Design* special issue *Folding in Architecture*, devoted in large measure to cataloging the architectural implications of Gilles Deleuze's concept of "the fold."[1] Part of a larger shift within architectural theory away from an interest in deconstruction and the work of Jacques Derrida, the folded projects and essays collected in *Folding in Architecture* offer examples of a new design technique that, as guest editor Greg Lynn suggests, departs from a deconstructivist "logic of conflict and contradiction" in order to develop "a more fluid logic of connectivity." Lynn argues that unlike deconstructivist techniques which simply represent the preexistent difference between a given form and its context, this new, folded design strategy offers a way to design heterogeneous yet coherent folded forms that do not represent but instead affiliate or link together differences between forms and their contexts. As Lynn notes, "If there is a single effect produced in architecture by folding, it will be the ability to integrate unrelated elements within a new continuous mixture"(8). As a result, the hard diagonals of deconstructivist architecture give way to more supple and affiliative folded forms, including the curvilinear roof of Frank Gehry's Guggenheim Museum in Bilbao, Spain, which Lynn suggests "integrates the large rectilinear masses of gallery and support space with the scale of the pedestrian and automotive contexts"; Peter Eisenman's Rebstock Park project, in which the fold is manifest in "the incorporation of differences—derived from the morphology of the site—into the homogeneous typologies of the housing and office blocks"; and, RAAUM's Croton Aqueduct project, which, following a single subterranean water supply for New York City, is "pulled through multiple disparate programs which are adjacent to and which cross it." But does this shift from deconstructivist forms to folded forms qualify as new?

Deleuze has not only given us the concept of the fold, but, with his provocative distinction between the *realization of the possible* and the *actualization of the virtual*, he has also given us a way to determine its usefulness for architecture. Deleuze makes this distinction in order to differentiate between two kinds of multiplicity: one that is redundant and one that is creative. The realization of the possible operates by the principles of limitation and resemblance. Since there are many possibles, any realization of any one of them necessarily limits these potential possibles to only one. But more importantly, since the possible comes to completion only by crossing over to realization, by being figured or represented as realization, and thus filling the hollow or gap that difference resides in, nothing new is created. In the circuit of the realization of the possible there exists a kind of preformism in which everything is already given in the possible so that nothing new is created in its realization. There is thus no difference between the possible and its realization, and without difference, without the interval between, the new cannot take form. There is perhaps no better example of this than the representation of theoretical and philosophical concepts in architectural form, as was the case, for example, with much of so-called deconstructivist architecture, and as appears to be the case with certain folded architectures. When a theoretical concept (the fold) or reading/writing protocol (deconstruction) is used as a blueprint to generate an architectural form, architecture becomes applied philosophy, and necessarily gives up all claims to singularity and creativity. The actualization of the virtual, on the other hand, does not operate by resemblance or representation, but by differentiation, divergence, and creation. As Deleuze observes: "In order to be actualized, the virtual cannot proceed by elimination or limitation, but must create its own lines of actualization in positive acts. The reason for this is simple: While the real is in the image and likeness of the possible that it realizes, the actual, on the other hand, does not resemble the virtuality it embodies. It is difference that is primary in the process of actualization—the difference between the virtual from which we begin and the actuals at which we arrive."[2] With the realization of the possible we witness the representation or figuration of what already is (since the idea of the possible is always taken from the real), and in the actualization of the virtual the becoming-other of something that, though real, has not yet been.

With Deleuze's distinction between the possible-real and the virtual-actual in mind, we should ask: does "the fold" contribute to the production of new forms of architecture, or does it simply repeat what already exists? Does it realize the possible by representing or figuring a concept (the fold) in (folded) architectural form, or does it actualize the virtual and create new, experimental, and unpredictable forms of architecture? To answer this we need to distinguish between a (folded) architectural form that is produced by representing a concept (the fold) and the form of a folded architectural practice. This is important, for as with the numerous other catalogings of new schools or groupings of architecture according to form—Jeffrey Kipnis's InFormation/DeFormation in *Folding in Architecture* being the most recent and one of the most interesting—what is overlooked is the significant matter of new forms of architectural practice itself, which, as Henri Focillon suggests of all of life, has a certain shape, a certain form that is the result of its affiliations and interminglings with other forms.[3] It is in the shaping of the form of practices (including techniques and logics), rather than the shaping of individual architectural forms, that the concept of the fold becomes important for the development of new architectural form. Alain Badiou has observed of Deleuze's concept of the fold that "Deleuze intends to follow Leibniz in his most paradoxical undertaking: establish the monad as 'absolute interiority' and go on to the most rigorous analysis possible of the relation of exteriority (or possession), in particular the relation between mind and body. Treating the outside as an exact reversion, or 'membrane,' of the inside, reading the world as a texture of the intimate, thinking the macroscopic (or the molar) as a torsion of the microscopic (or the molecular): these are undoubtedly the operations that constitute the true effectiveness of the concept of Fold."[4] A practice that operates by folding would necessarily fold this relationship (and not represent a neo-baroque form) into the shape or form of its own practice, thus actualizing the virtual concept of the fold—for it too must be understood as an external, a force whose greatest effect is not its representability in form, but its potential to shape the form of practice. Thus new forms of architecture will not emerge as a result of the effects achieved by ever more pliant, fluid, complex, and heterogeneous shapes or architectural forms, but rather with the development of more pliant, complex, and heterogeneous forms of architectural practice—with architectural practices supple enough to be formed by what is outside or external to them, yet resilient enough to retain their coherence as architecture.

One such folded architectural practice is that of Parisian furniture designer/architect Bernard Cache. For Cache, whose work has developed in close proximity to Deleuze's philosophy seminar in Paris, the fold expresses a relationship between the exterior (geography) and the interior (furniture) of architecture. Following Deleuze's assertion that "the interior is only a selected exterior, and the exterior a projected interior," Cache employs the fold as a way to rethink the relationship between body and soul, past and present, and between furniture, architecture, and geography.

Cache redefines architecture not only by rethinking its relationship with its exterior and interior, but also, following Henri Bergson and Deleuze, by rethinking the very nature of this interior and exterior world as one made of images. Developing a new understanding of the architectural image, Cache describes *Earth Moves* as a classifier of images: "We wish to classify the images that make up our everyday lives, and, among these, architectural images seem to be a good starting point, as they in fact determine the urban texture that enfolds all other images." For Cache, architectural images are not second-order reflections of an exterior reality but are themselves constituents of a primary world, in which the human brain is a special kind of image. As he writes, "Our brain is not the seat of a neuronal cinema that reproduces the world; rather our perceptions are inscribed on the surface of things, as images amongst images." This image world precedes man and cannot be controlled or limited by representation or figuration of a more primary, Platonic, humanistic world. Resistant to the fixation and limitation of Cartesian spatial coordinates, this temporal, image milieu is a dynamical, variable world in which new movements and creations emerge in the intercalary spaces between images. It is for this reason that Cache redefines architecture as the art of the frame: architecture thus escapes its traditional role of housing and grounding and becomes a practice of framing images in such a way that they induce new forms of life. Taking advantage of these intercalar spaces, these intervals of life-creating indeterminacy, architecture first isolates (by way of the wall), selects (using the device of the window) one of these intervals from the external topography, and then arranges this interval in such a way as to increase the probability of an intended effect. Taken all together, these three activities—isolating, selecting, and arranging—delimit Cache's redefined architectural practice of enframing, of which Deleuze has written: "Interlocking these frames or joining up all these planes—wall section, window section, floor section, slope section—is a composite system rich in points and counterpoints. The frames and their joins hold the compounds of sensations, hold up figures, and intermingle with their upholding, their own appearance."[5]

Following this redefinition of architecture, Cache, in one of the most provocative chapters in *Earth Moves*, develops a reevaluation of perspective by framing an image of the exterior topography of an apartment in Montreux through the device of the window, which is then folded into the apartment, rendering what was exterior part of the interior, and what was interior coexistent with the exterior. What emerges from this process is a more fluid logic of involuted sacks rather than boxes: "A contains B, which doesn't prevent B from being able to contain A. The window frames the landscape as much as the landscape encompasses the frame." This same logic pertains at the even more intimate level of the furniture image, which Cache argues is not only an interior replication of architecture—the closet is a box within a box and the table is simply an elevated floor—but the primary territory of the body. The furniture image is thus the hinge point between geography and architecture. For Cache the conditions for the new in architecture are created on this virtual hinge point, which he calls the "inflection image," a special image that Deleuze has noted "is essential to any theory of the fold."[6] Indeed, it is the inflection image that connects Cache's two redefinitions of architecture—as a folded practice of interior and exterior relations and as the art of the frame. It is only by selecting these continuously variable image points that we gain access to the virtual, which is for Cache the only condition under which new architecture emerges. Indeed, it is perhaps on this inflection point that architecture can become other, can become new, and survive its own entropic conservatism.

Today we must acknowledge that any new form of architecture (folded or otherwise) will not only have to rethink the specific forms it produces, but, as a condition for doing so, will have to rethink the form, shape, and articulation of its practice of architecture. Folded forms may be one result of this attempt—they are not exclusive to a folded practice. On the other hand, it may be that the fold has only the limited use of providing certain architectural practices with theoretical cachet. But one asks these questions in the belief that not only the fold but Deleuze's pragmatic constructivism has a great deal to offer architecture. More than this can only be developed when architecture is made to think its outside, to become other, to become new. Only then will it take new forms.

Michael Speaks

1. *Folding in Architecture*, ed. Greg Lynn (London: Architectural Design, 1993).

2. Gilles Deleuze, *Bergsonism*, trans. Hugh Tomlinson and Barbara Habberjam (New York: Zone Books, 1988), 97.

3. See Henri Focillon, *The Life of Forms*, trans. Charles Beecher Hogan and George Kubler (New York: Zone Books, 1989).

4. *Gilles Deleuze and the Theatre of Philosophy*, ed. Constantin Boundas and Dorothea Olkowski (New York: Routledge Books, 1994), 61.

5. Gilles Deleuze and Félix Guattari, *What Is Philosophy?*, trans. Hugh Tomlinson and Graham Burchell (New York: Columbia University Press, 1994), 187.

6. See Gilles Deleuze, *The Fold: Leibniz and the Baroque*, trans. Tom Conley (Minneapolis: University of Minnesota Press).

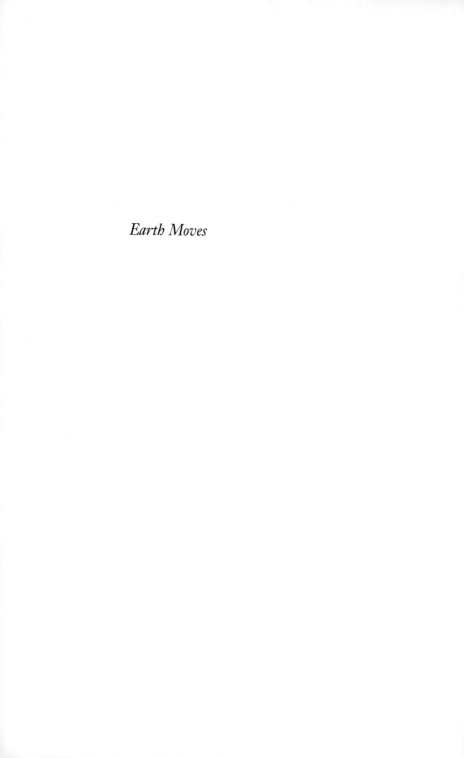

Earth Moves

This book is a classifier of images. We wish to classify the images that make up our everyday lives, and, among these, architectural images seem to be a good starting point, as they in fact determine the urban texture that enfolds all other images.

We will first consider the word "image" in its traditional sense, which is to say: a simple visual document. In the elaboration of an architectural project, the image is the series of documents that starts with the location plan, leads to sketches, and ends up with the building plans. As we examine these images, we come to see that they correspond, successively, to three formal elements: inflection, vector, and frame.

These three elements then allow us to classify images in a wider sense: they are no longer only documents but are any visible object, and in particular those objects that are involved in an aesthetic endeavor. We will then see that it is possible to define architecture as the manipulation of one of these elementary images, namely, the frame. Architecture, the art of the frame, would then not only concern those specific objects that are buildings, but would refer to any image involving any element of framing, which is to say painting as well as cinema, and certainly many other things. An assertion of this kind will of course have to be tested by reference to art history.

Our examination will then first be a critical one. We will try to see in what way our three elements allow for a formal reading of works of the past. Inflection, vector, and frame would constitute an alphabet whose rules are never determined but are always determinable, as they are always present in the images that have been elaborated throughout the ages, even if each period, each artist, or each work emphasizes one or another of these elements and must each time invent its own modes of configuration.

In the second place, our examination will have a practical end. The question will then be to see to what extent our elements might allow us not only to read the works of the past but to understand those of the present, and, we hope, to prepare us for those of the future. We have now been through a long critical phase of the modern movement, but might we not find in it something today that could offer us the bases of a new constructivism? Are the inflections that seem to be cropping up here and there in contemporary architecture merely anecdotal? Or are they the herald of an aesthetic that is necessarily new, since modes of production have changed, but that is still essentially modern, since they seem to represent a fresh attempt to synthesize the formal, the social, and the technical? Moreover, do numerical technologies not give us the tools to realize once again Leibniz's program: "Everything can be calculated"? Neo-constructivism, neo-baroque: these terms are not postmodern quotations; they refer to the power of ideal events that no realization can ever exhaust and that will always return.

Finally, we can give the image its widest meaning, designating thereby anything that presents itself to the mind, "whether it be real or not." In this way, we pass from visible objects to visibility itself. The word "image" then places us in a purely optical register where effects are produced without reference to any given object. But these effects are not deceptive illusions, for perception is not an interior image of exterior objects but stands for things themselves. Our brain is not the seat of a neuronal cinema that reproduces the world; rather our perceptions are inscribed on the surface of things, as images amongst images. We ourselves would be nothing other than these optical haloes that are drawn at the intersection of the radii of curvature that fold the surface of images. Whence the interest of a classification.

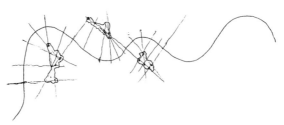

one **Territorial Image**

Topography is a primary concern in the establishment of cities. Thucydides had already referred to this problem, stating it in terms of the dilemma that faced the Greek polis: ancient cities had to secure a position of retreat on a defensive site as well as a position of communication on a site that was easily accessible. Thus Athens would be split into two, as it installed the polis on the hill of the Parthenon and the port in the cove of Piraeus. This is a simplistic way of presenting the problem, however, for history itself usually multiplies the sites of urban implantation according to the shifting relations between a city and its territory. The best example might be a city that is rich in geography: Lausanne.

Located along the shores of Lac Léman, the present city of Lausanne stretches between a green plane formed by the extremity of the Swiss plateau and a blue plane drawn by the surface of the lake. The connection between the two has never been a simple matter, and it is just the problem Jean-Luc Godard focused on in his short film on Lausanne: how do you get from the green plane of the hills to the blue plane of the lake? It is a pictorial problem "à la Cézanne," says Godard, but it is also a geological one: the glacier of the Rhône deposited lateral moraines along the shores of the lake in such a way that they impede the run of the waters on the hillside. Most of the rivers are thus diverted from their fall line and have to find a weak spot in the moraine before they can flow into the lake.

Moreover, the site of Lausanne is not divided by one waterway but by two, the Flon and the Louve, that carve out, higher up than their point of confluence,

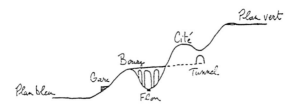

steep slopes on a spur of molasse. The complexity of the site accounts for the building of many artworks: tunnels and bridges, stairs and elevators, funiculars and supporting walls that ensure an urban continuity between these diverse geographical terrains. But above all, each of these constructs is the sign of an intervention in a site, the reading of which has varied throughout its history.

The first traces of settling on the Lausanne site are to be found on the alluvial beach formed at the mouth of the Flon. Archaeologists believe they have discovered, along with prehistoric structures, the remains of a Gallo-Roman port. This choice of a site easily accessed by lake and by land coincided with the favorable historical conditions of the *pax romana*: security of transport and political stability. In some sense, this Gallo-Roman Lausanne prefigured the settling of the touristic site beneath the sunny hillside, in Ouchy, a century ago.

And yet, during the fourth century, this pleasing lake site was ignored in favor of the rocky spur where the cathedral now stands. It is hard to know whether this displacement was due to an onslaught of bandits or to a tidal wave caused by the collapse of a mountainside into the lake. But the choice of a narrow and inaccessible site such as the molassic spur certainly satisfied concerns of a strategic order, even if it was also to be thought suitable for the expression of spiritual elevation and thus for the building of the cathedral. Following the example of many other medieval towns, Lausanne then presented itself as a city perched on a mountaintop.

Facing the narrow spur of the Cité, the crest formed by the glacial moraine represented a natural communication route. This crest can be read in two ways depending on which axis is considered: the transverse section reveals an apex that emerges from the wooded and hesitant slopes of the hillside, while the longitudinal section shows a gently sloping link between the level of the lake and that of the Jorat (the blue and green planes Godard referred to). This double reading would allow the crest to become a primary communication route between Bern and Geneva. Merchants quickly settled at the top of the ancient moraine and a new site, the Bourg, was established. Even today, one of the busiest commercial streets of Lausanne is to be found along this crest line. But during the Middle Ages, these two sites were still segregated and the commercial Bourg confronted the episcopal Cité; between the two, the valley of the Flon separated the rocky spur from the morainic crest. Only later would this valley become populated. For the river, no longer only a waterway, also became a source of motor energy for a whole set of proto-industrial activities: mills, sawmills, and belt factories. Despite their rivalry, it then became necessary to ensure communication between the Bourg and the Cité, and all the more so because the narrowness of the latter soon forced it to spread onto the slopes of the Flon's tributary. At first, however, the inhabitants of the valley formed a distinct group, calling itself "Community of the lower city." It was only in 1481 that the three cities were united under the same banner. Later, in 1555, a vaulting was built over the Flon. The Place du Pont,

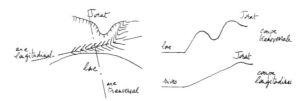

designed at that time, consecrated the role of the Flon in the Lausanne conglomeration.

In 1803, Lausanne was elected capital of the canton of Vaud, thus perpetuating its episcopal vocation. Administrative and commercial activities developed and the need for improving the urban infrastructures was felt.

To the narrowness and winding characteristic of medieval sites was added the tortuousness of the local terrain. The extreme variations in level and the greatest inclines had to be eliminated. The question was then how to select a gently sloping plane of transport that would bypass the difficult geographical terrain formed by the spur of the Cité as well as the bottom of the valley of the Flon. The building of a tunnel and two large-scale bridges would establish the level of a midplane that could regulate car traffic. What is now known as the Ceinture Pichard thus traverses the spur of the Cité, crosses the Flon valley, and joins the crest line of the Bourg.

Furthermore, the industrial revolution marked its presence through the creation of a railway. But because of its terrain, Lausanne was first declared a city "out of reach by rail." Thus the first line to link Morges and Yverdon only serviced Lausanne in a secondary way, and even then it stopped only in Renens, which is below the city. A federal decision had to be reached before Lausanne was integrated into the railroad network. Once again, the terrain of Lausanne had to be reckoned with. Two options were considered: a terminal station in the Flon valley with a backup point under the Grand Pont, or else a thoroughfare station on the hillside below the Bourg.

Les alternatives ferroviaires : gare terminus gare de passage

In 1856, the second option prevailed. The plane of the Ceinture Pichard would then stretch along the Léman hillside, linking the station to the city. The construction of this Pichard plane was to reshape the entire organization of the city, marginalizing all the neighborhoods that were either above or below it. Still today, the collective memory of Lausanne is structured by this plane that creates a sort of split: on either side of the plane, different social groups make use of the terrain in very different ways. While most inhabitants tend to go out of their way to avoid climbing up to the Cité, or worse still, going down into the Flon valley, certain groups particularly choose those locations. Disreputable neighborhoods, warehouses that shelter industrial as well as other, more illicit, activities, have become the fate of the bottom of the valley; so much so that subway users rush to get on the public elevator to join the level of the Ceinture Pichard on the Grand Pont. On the other hand, the Cité has become a historical center, much to the delight of a handful of civil servants and students of classical letters. The cathedral is thus the counterpart of Ouchy on the lake shore, that other place away from the traffic of the Ceinture Pichard; they are the two picture postcards of the city: the lake and the Cité.

This formalist history of Lausanne should suffice to put into question the notion of urban identity. For far from expressing the "nature" of a place, the identity of a city is eminently variable and assumes the most diverse forms. In the case of the city of Lausanne, at least four distinct figures can be counted:

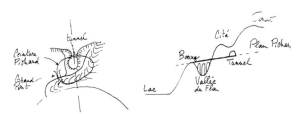

- the perched Cité,
- the city of the Bourg crest,
- the city of the valley that stretches along the Flon,
- the city of the Léman slope surrounded by the
  Ceinture Pichard.

For each of these urban identities, a geometrical figure can be drawn: a cone for the perched city, an inclined prism for the crest city, a dihedral for the valley, and a plane that stretches toward the lake for the sloped city. A sort of cubist sculpture of the city of Lausanne could then be constructed through the combination of these four basic figures: cone, prism, dihedral, and plane.[1]

This sculpture is a mnemotechnical object. One must also remember that the surface of the territory is mobile and fluid as it is given to the continual distortions of memory. Thus each of the four figures might be said to consolidate a singular distortion of the relief of the city. If a section of the terrain of Lausanne is effectuated along the axis of the transept of the cathedral, the resulting abstract line can become a point of reference. We discover once again the blue and green planes between which the principal geographic configurations of the city can be found: the slope, the crest, the valley, and the spur. Starting from this characteristic outline, we can also draw four diagrams that offer as many readings of the site. Each diagram translates the action of a vector that folds the abstract line of the terrain. But what is the nature of this vector?

On each diagram thus folded, the vector expresses a way of raising the problem of topography. The series of

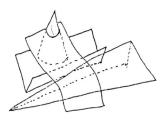

diagrams indicate the different ways in which this question has been posed throughout history. These are the strategic concerns at the time of the Cité, the Geneva-Bern connection during the era of the Bourg, the securing of motor energy for the Community of the lower city, and finally, the selection of a gently sloping mid-plane for Pichard.

But very quickly, it becomes clear that this series of vectors does not translate a simple historical succession. First of all, because during each period many secondary concerns confer additional values to each of these vectors. Thus we mentioned that the vertical vector of the Cité carried religious or political significance as well as a strategic one. The same is true of the three other vectors. It does not even seem useful to arrange these values in a hierarchy, for the significant distinction occurs between an abstract vectorial space and the concrete values that are projected onto it.

More precisely, the first four historical concerns that have been described can all be translated into gravitational terms: letting stones fall, climbing a hill, positioning oneself on the thalweg, or choosing the least inclined plane. What counts, in fact, is the reading of a territory in terms of a conjunction between two sorts of images: concrete gravitational vectors and abstract vectorial space. It makes no difference that religious elevation may be very different from physical gravity; it doesn't prevent these two images from being grafted onto one another, because they are two images that have the same formal characteristics: they are two vector images.

Each abstract vector nails down a multiplicity of concrete values, such that the historical succession of vectors appears as a sort of repetition. It's not because of any *genius loci* that the cathedral's spire still preserves

Diagramme 1

Diagramme 2

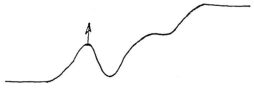

Diagramme 3

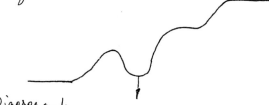

Diagramme 4

its meaning; it is rather that the abstract vector of the site still designates the Cité as a place of predilection, whether as a seat for the Vaud parliament or as the place for local festivities. And in the same way, one must not be surprised to find traffic jams today on the site of the Gallo-Roman forum, for it still offers the same singular configuration with respect to the gravitational vector: as it is at the intersection of the horizontal plane of the lake and the thalweg of the Flon valley, it is the mouth of the waterway.

But even beyond repetition, one must learn to read a space of "transistance" that allows us to pass from one vector to another. Throughout the ages, the identity of Lausanne has not so much changed, or repeated itself, as it has lived with itself under the determination of these four sorts of vectors. It would still be possible for us today to relate each of these urban identities to the diverse communities that make up the city as well as to the individual consciousness of its inhabitants. The problem is not so much that of the collective or individual memory that sustains these identities as that of the coexistence of these four apparently incompatible urban figures that are the cone, the prism, the dihedral, and the plane. The real question is then to find a solution of contiguity between these four geometrical figures; it is a question of deploying a space of transistance from one identity to another.

It is also a question of craft. In the exercise of their profession, architects can choose to ground their practice in the concept of site. The work of architecture then becomes the expression of the specificity of the site that is to be built upon. This has in fact been the option of a number of architects, of whom Vittorio Gregotti is probably the best contemporary example. But this position runs the danger of falling into a mistaken notion of site, equating all too easily the notion of specificity with that of identity. The case of Lausanne demonstrates clearly enough that the identity of a place is not given, and that if the expression "genius loci" has a meaning, it lies in the capacity of this "genius" to be smart enough to allow for the transformation or transit from one identity to another. These four figures of Lausanne are virtualities that each architect can decide to ignore or to actualize as he or she formulates his or her project for the city. Lining up cornices for the Pichard plan, or paving the boulevard along the bottom of the valley, are gestures through which an architect can position him or herself with respect to a site. But in no case does the identity of a site preexist, for it is always the outcome of a construction.

Generally, today, it no longer seems possible to think in terms of identity. Whether it refers to the identity of a place or of a self, a substantialist way of thinking seems to lead to a dead end. For as soon as one attributes a particular identity to a particular place, the only possible modes of intervention then become imitation, dissimulation, or minimalism. A false notion of the past prevents the present from happening. A difficult position must then be maintained: between, on one hand, the desire to make use of the specificity of the place, and on the other, the danger of "identifying" local differences. Opting for difference only becomes tenable when one learns how to distinguish specificity and identity.

This task of working beneath the surface of identities has been a focus of recent philosophy. For the most part, however, this sort of work has only served to renew the practices of negative theology. According to this way of thinking, language belongs to the "identical," and thus any discourse that is held "beneath" it can only proceed through negation or reduction. In architectural theory, this gives rise to statements such as "reinforce the identity of a place," which implicitly means that identity is not given and must be constructed; but in fact identity is already there, and has only to be emphasized. The specificity of a place would thus only be its unaffirmed identity.

For example, the Great Wall of China is merely thought to have underscored a natural crest line that prefigured the territorial identity of the Middle Empire. But if we look at the historical variations of this line, we see that the wall constantly fluctuated under the pressure exerted by the Mongols. There was no line present at the start that only needed reinforcing. We must thus develop a positive mode of thinking that is prior to identities but that does not resort to the indeterminate, the informal, the nonverbal. We believe that certain images can become crystal-clear while never entering into the order of the identical.

Take the concept of singularity. In mathematics, what is said to be singular is not a given point, but rather a set of points on a given curve. A point is not singular; it becomes singularized on a continuum. And several types of singularity exist, starting with fractures in curves and other bumps in the road. We will discount them at the outset, for singularities that are marked by discontinuity signal events that are exterior to the curvature and are themselves easily identifiable. In the same way, we will eliminate singularities such as backup points [*points de rebroussement*]. For though they are indeed discontinuous, they refer to a vector that is tangential to the curve and thus trace a symmetrical axis that is constitutive of the backup point. Whether it be a reflection of the tangential plane or a rebound with respect to the orthogonal plane, the backup point is thus not a basic singularity. It is rather the result of an operation effectuated on any part of the curve. Here again, the singular would be the sign of too noisy, too memorable an event, while what we want to do is to deal with what is most *smooth*: ordinary continua, sleek and polished.

We will then retain two types of singularity. On one hand there are the extrema, the maximum and minimum on a given curve. And on the other there are those singular points that, in relation to the extrema, figure as in-betweens. These are known as points of inflection. They are different from the extrema in that they are defined only in relation to themselves, whereas the definition of the extrema presupposes the prior choice of an axis or an orientation, that is to say of a vector.

Indeed, a maximum or a minimum is a point where the tangent to the curve is directed perpendicularly to the axis of the ordinates [*y*-axis]. Any new orientation of the coordinate axes repositions the maxima and the minima; they are thus extrinsic singularities. The point of inflection, however, designates a pure event of curvature where the tangent crosses the curve; yet this event does not depend in any way on the orientation of the axes, which is why it can be said that inflection is an intrinsic singularity. On either side of the inflection, we know that there will be a highest point and a lowest point, but we cannot designate them as long as the curve has not been related to the orientation of a vector. Points of inflection are singularities in and of themselves, while they confer an indeterminacy to the rest of the curve. Preceding the vector, inflection makes of each of the points a possible extremum in relation to its inverse: virtual maxima and minima. In this way, inflection represents a totality of possibilities, as well as an openness, a receptiveness, or an anticipation.

We are thus faced with three types of images or concepts: inflections, vectors, and the geometrical figures of identity. They are three sorts of images that are superimposed in the constitution of a territory, where each refers to a different level of reading. We have already reviewed the cubist composition of the identities of Lausanne and the vectorial diagrams of the enfoldings of memory. We are now confronted with a very peculiar image. It is that of the inflections of the relief of Lausanne: the orographic map.

This map is a pure form because on its surface no signs or markings appear at all. The orographic design is a design without destiny, a map without a plan. A world before man, even if we know that it is man-made. For we will see that this surface has the strange quality of being first though it is constructed and is never fully realized. What is this image? As it has no value, it has nothing obscure; as it has no meaning, it has no top or bottom, right or left; as it has no density, it is superficial, which is to say geographical and not geological; and as it has no center, its boundaries are nowhere, for any scansion would allow for meaning to emerge and would constitute objects and singularities through discontinuity. In short, it is an open surface in the pure light of weightlessness. It is like a thin film whose neutrality is reminiscent of the monochrome objects of Kurt Schwitters.

It might be said, of course, that orographic maps nevertheless comprise contour lines that still have to do with the orientation of gravitational vectors. That is because the map that we see is already no longer first, but that is a lesser evil. It is inevitable that what is first must yield, and either allow its surface to be covered with signs or else vanish. When faced with a surface of variable curvature, we necessarily focus on its extrinsic singularities. All we see are highs and lows. Among geographical documents, only orographic maps lead our eye toward inflections, for the contour lines are concentrat-

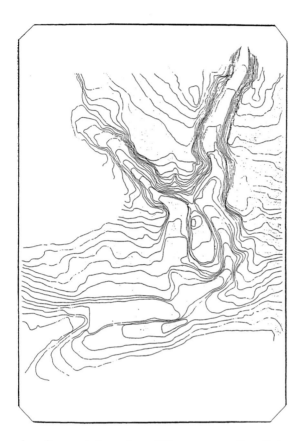

ed or dispersed about them. What we normally call the maximum slope line is in fact no such thing. For the thalweg, the line where the waters gather, is the line of an equilibrium restored, a twin line around which the river that seeks its course fluctuates. But the point of imbalance, the point of incline, is the point of inflection. In planar projection, it is the area where the contour lines are concentrated. Or, under another definition, the point of inflection becomes the point of a plateau from which the contour lines diverge. These are the facts that language betrays but that orographic maps display.

two **Architectural Image**

An architectural practice that deals with the problem of site thus brings three basic images into play: the site plan (the orographic map), the vectorial sketch (the folded diagram), and finally those geometrical figures (cone, dihedron, prism, and plane) that give a cubist appearance to any urban composition. The fundamental component of such a composition is certainly the edifice, but beyond those concrete buildings that house our everyday lives, can we find an abstract principle that specifies the nature of this third register of images? In other words, what is "the architectural" in an edifice?

We can begin to answer this question by noting that, strictly speaking, architects design frames. This can be easily verified by consulting architectural plans, which are nothing but the interlocking of frames in every dimension: plans, sections, and elevations. Cubes, nothing but cubes. Architects have certainly been blamed enough for this. But we have to know what it is we are talking about and define the frame more precisely. In the first place, the term can be understood according to its most common meaning: a frame is four wooden sticks surrounding a picture. The model of architectural form would thus be the frame of a painting. In a text called "Déblaiements d'art," Henry Van de Velde pointed to a parallelism between the historical evolution of the shapes of the frames and that of architectural forms. Paintings would finalize, as it were, the series of frames that make up a building. Through successive unframings, we would pass from the canvas of the painting to the fresco on the wall, to the mosaic on the ground, and finally to the stained glass in the window frame. Thus the frame of a painting would be a residual, or better yet, a rudiment of architectural framing.

The frame reduces architecture to its most basic expression and allows us to formulate a concept that derives directly from Eugène Dupréel, whose philosophy was centered entirely on the notion of frame of probability. Dupréel criticized the classical causal scheme, remarking that no value has been attributed to the interval that separates the cause from the realization of its effect. For a cause to produce an effect, this interval must be filled. For in and of themselves, the set of causes that produce an effect are only frames of probability. One never knows how the interval will be filled; otherwise, everything that is known about the interval would cross over to the side of the cause, and all one would have done is to define a more restricted frame of probability. And if, by any chance, no indeterminacy remained in the interval, the cause would become identical to the effect and nothing new could happen at all. Eugène Dupréel's philosophy is interesting in that it is essentially realistic. What most rationalists say is: "We know that things don't occur exactly in this way, but we will assume that, in all likelihood, they do." To which Dupréel answers: "Be realistic, do not ignore the interval that is a basic component of causality." Experimental imprecision, the occurrence of unexpected events, are the signs that reality is a hollow image and that its structure is alveolar. Intervals always remain and intercalated phenomena always slip into them, even if they finally break the frames of probability apart.

In return, this intercalar dimension of reality allows us to reformulate a rationalist theory of architectural practice. Architecture would be the art of introducing intervals in a territory in order to construct frames of probability. This presupposes that the architectural frame fulfill at least three functions, whatever the concrete purpose of the building might be.

The first function is that of separation. Its functional element is the wall. One must delimit an interval in which a form of life that doesn't fit a priori in its milieu will occur. For life naturally transpires in the intervals of matter. Life is that intercalar phenomenon that causes alone can never produce; at best, we can try to circumscribe frames of probability. The causes of life always escape us, which is why we can only provide niches in which it can take place. It is as if life could not even coexist with itself and only progressed by entrenchments. If we wish to define architecture as an operation on space, we must then define the nature of this space more precisely. Classical philosophy saw it as a form of coexistence or simultaneity. It was contrasted with time, which was seen as a form of succession. But architectural space is not this general form of simultaneity; it is a space where coexistence is not a fundamental given, but rather the uncertain outcome of processes of separation and partitioning. The wall is the basis of our coexistence. Architecture builds its space of compatibility on a mode of discontinuity.

The second abstract function of the frame is selection. The frame thus becomes a window that carefully selects the causes of life in order to produce ever more singular effects. The first function of the frame removed us from the territory; the second function reestablishes connections, selectively. This becomes clear in relation to the image of the folded diagram mentioned above. The abstract line of the section of the territory confronts a multiplicity of possible vectors. Circumstances determine which vector will assume a particular importance, after which the points of the curve will organize around the designation of the maxima and the minima. One point will become the apex, while another will indicate the thalweg. But since all vectors are given at the outset, and since their relative significance is extremely variable, to stop at one, or at several, presupposes a process of selection.

The second function of the frame is to select the vector that will fold the abstract line and thus designate the apexes. According to the angle produced between a given vector and the frame, it will be said that such a location is more or less sunny, more or less windy, but mainly more or less singular. The frame operates on a vectorial multiplicity in order to determine its "bite" on the diagram. The image of a simple vector is thus never given without the frame image which selects it being constituted at the same time. The wall delimits dark rooms; the window lets the sun shine in; what is still needed is a surface that stretches its screen to the variable play of shadows formed by the light.

Once the interval is delimited and the vector selected, this interval must be arranged in such a way as to allow the frame of probability to produce its effects. The interval is a factor of absolute uncertainty. But from the causes that have been selected, one can increase the probability of an expected effect by eliminating all disturbances in the interval. Thus rationality proceeds in a dual manner: on one hand, causes are selected more and more carefully; on the other, the interval is arranged in such a way as to eliminate all intercalar phenomena. As metals and ceramics are being extended and tarmac and linoleum are spread everywhere, how can we fail to notice this increase of smooth and rarefied surfaces? Even before pressurized laboratories or factories, architecture was creating these smooth intervals that increase the probability of emergence of new forms of life.

It is the flatness of the stage that makes choreography probable, just as it is the flatness of the stadium that increases the probability of athletics. The ground plane rarefies the surface of the earth in order to allow human activities to take shape. But as these surfaces become increasingly smooth and continuous, their grip is reduced to a minimum. The stairway becomes a ramp and the ground falls away. As trajectories become more precise, the slightest protrusion induces slippages. Such is the nature of the modern interval: movement on a rarefied ground that turns into an aberration. A whole range of dynamic states are thus produced, of which Francis Bacon's paintings may be a sort of demonstration. The first state is a basic free fall: popes fall into the void as if they were experiments in gravity; the frame encloses an interval of rarefied air in which all resistance is eliminated. The second dynamic state is more formal, as centrifugal energy becomes a transportational vector that is orthogonal to the circular trajectory. This allows for otherwise impossible movements to occur, such as a foot seizing a key in the *Triptique* of 1974. And finally, the true nature of the aberration of modern movement: the absence of trajectory allows for impossible recoveries on a smooth background of nonadherence, as in *Figure in Movement* of 1976.

Walls, windows, floors: the box is almost closed. But what about the roof? Of course, the roof protects; it delimits and selects. As such the roof is but a horizontal wall and presents no specificity at all. And indeed, a certain type of modern architecture placed a box on stilts, a box with no top or bottom, whose flat roof would be no different from the walls and the floors. Did Le Corbusier not say of the Villa Savoye that he intended to eliminate all notions of "front" and "back," and wished only to create a "box in the air"?[2] But in this case, what is the specificity of the older sloping roof? We must see that in all instances, the roof belonged to a specific formal register: the prism, the dome, the cone, the pyramid. Here we encounter once again the figures of territorial identity, as well as the crest line or apex: the figures of extrinsic singularity. The frame of probability selects a vector and produces site as singularity. The pyramid is the eminent figure of the singular as extremum. The sloping roof then differs from the three other elements of the frame, for it is neither an interval nor a cause; it is the envelope of an effect: it is the singular becoming of a place, of the domestic as an eminent place.

What then happens when modern architects reduce the roof to the status of walls? The house loses its bearings and each stone becomes a potential floor. The window stretches out lengthwise and becomes panoramic. This window no longer frames the zenith; it is now a "distributor of light." No longer does the sun, framed for but a few moments by the window, aim its rays at an immobilized dweller. This all too singular moment gives way to the shadings of variable light. As the roof becomes indifferent to verticality, the lengthened window no longer selects any particular orientation; it allows a certain degree of freedom to the multiple vectors of the course of the sun. As no precise orientation designates an extremum, eminence must yield to a more discrete, intrinsic singularity. What has happened to the roof in modern architecture? It followed the same path as singularity. It went from being exterior to being interior. The roof axis is given over to the inflection of the free plane. The edge of the prism disappears into the box, becomes incurved as it follows the walls of variable curvature, coils up into the helicoidal line of a stairway, and sculpts a spine in the bathroom of the Villa Savoye.

The sloping roof constructed place in terms of eminence; implicitly, traditional edifices were therefore built on hilltops. Conversely, the natural location of the modern edifice is the midslope. It looks as though, perched on stilts, modernity had been looking for the maximal incline as a technical challenge made possible by reinforced concrete. But the flat roof is mainly a sign that

Les sites implicites de l'architecture :
1° traditionnel   2° moderne

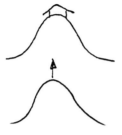

beneath the modern edifice, the point of slope is a point of inflection that places the edifice outside of the slope. The modern frame encloses the sloping point but no longer designates a single vector. The multiplicity of vectors returns the slope to its intrinsic singularity. The ground plane, now standing on stilts, introduces a slippage in the inflection of the relief.

The wall delimits and the window selects: such is the frame of probability within which we find the rarefied interval of the floor. It belongs to the regime of causes and of the interval. The roof is of another order: it envelops an event; it is the effect of singularization. So far, we have only spoken of abstract functions and have not considered any concrete content. We have dealt neither with form nor with the function of the edifice. This is because the notion of frame of probability presupposes that a distance or dehiscence be maintained between a frame and its content: one never knows how the interval that is marked off by the frame will be filled. This radical incongruence between a frame and its content explains why the concrete function of so many buildings is so easily transformed: a church becomes a market; a school becomes a hospital. The same frame selects the same vectorial diagram, but in the interval the effect has changed.

In the most general terms, functionalism in architecture means that the form serves the function. Very often this is understood as meaning that form should coincide with function in the mode of a representative analogy or of a cinematic envelope. Yet in their everyday lives, dwellers are quite capable of carrying out their tasks; the frame is only there to make their completion more probable. A truly rationalist theory relegates architecture to the position of distant cause. Form frames function rather than compressing it as in a mold or reflecting it like a mirror. There is an essential difference between the frame of probability and the effect that is produced within it. This difference in kind between cause and effect prevents us from making congruent the frame and the function. The rigid form of the frame cannot coincide with that of an effect that is always subject to variations and is only probable. That is why the frame belongs to a register of autonomous forms whose principle must still be defined.

We are then back to thinking of form as form, which means that we take things as images, with no relation to depth, to anteriority, or to use, and even less to representation. We have already proposed the simple definition of territories as surfaces of variable curvature bearing diverse singularities. We will now consider architecture to be nothing but the interlocking of frames. We will also henceforth attribute to any given object the status of simple image. In view of this cinema of things, we can proceed to a classification and verify that, formally, a building is not the equivalent of an object or a territory. And that therefore architecture, design, and the planning of territories require different skills, though all three work with form. For one can never tell what one draws, and there are plenty of examples of architectural objects, of geographized buildings, or of objectal territories. We might then think of furniture images as mobile centers that appear at the intersection of these three perspectives. Though classified as objects in our everyday language, furniture can be seen as an interior replication of architecture. The closet is a box in the box, the mirror a window onto the outside, and the table another floor on the ground. But at the same time as it is a replication of architecture, furniture is also that object that is directly connected to our bodies. For our most intimate or most abstract endeavors, whether they occur in bed or on a chair, furniture supplies the immediate physical environment in which our bodies act and react; for us, urban animals, furniture is thus our primary territory. Architecture, object, geography—furniture is that image where forms are fused together, and that will thus enable us to proceed to a classification.

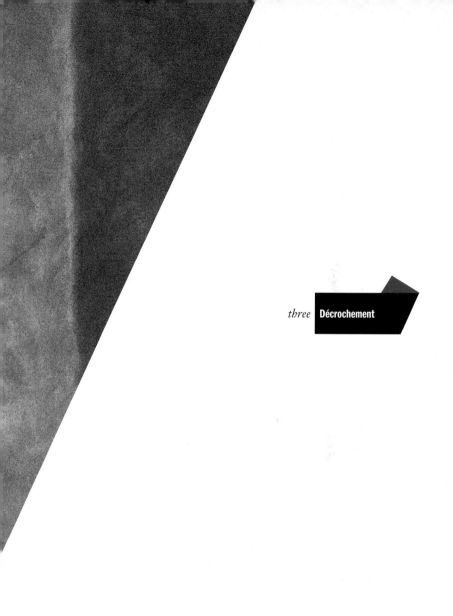

three **Décrochement**

This first piece of furniture is a wall fixture supporting two luminous sources. A metallic plate assembles a shade made of colored resin and a necklike shape carved out of a block of white marble. The resin shade has been poured into a mold constructed by a succession of strata. Thus even though the outside remains smooth, the inside has as many crenels as there are level lines on the mold. A more structured light can thus be obtained than the one that shines through the marble.

It can also be said that the metal plate introduces a gap in the line that connects the profile of the shade and that of the marble sculpture. Simply put, a hollow shape follows a hump; a minimum follows a maximum, which is to say that we find an inflection.

These slippages around a point of inflection are often found in baroque stylistic motifs. The inversion of the swirls generally coincides with a slippage at the point where the swirling movements are reversed. One might wonder whether this represents a fanciful excess, or whether it is rather a feature of inflection. The slippage is not added onto the inflection; it reveals its formal characteristics. In this way one could also come to see a precise connection between baroque style and the implicit site of modern architecture.

Let us now return to the mathematical classification of singularities. Inflection, which is intrinsic singularity, contrasts with those singularities that can only be specified after the determination of a vector. These latter singularities are the points said to be extrema: the maxima and the minima. In our daily lives, we are constantly confronted with extrema: the law of maximum slope, the maximization of profit, the shortest way, the least effort, the minimizing of stress, etc. Indeed, it would seem that we see nothing but these extrema, for our perception is

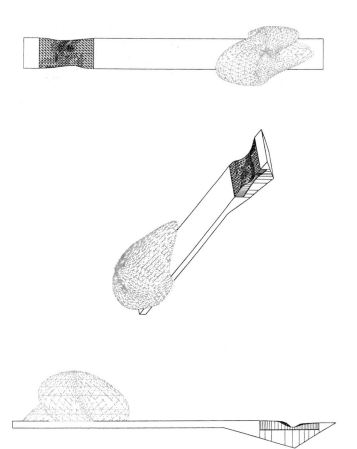

entirely oriented in this way. Orientation, structuring, selection, identification: in these ways perception is maximized according to the best response. It is not that nothing else is possible, but that all that is possible is reduced to that which is chosen in relation to the best. Leibniz had said so in his day: it's the law of the universe. So much so that we forget that the world is not all that is, and that maybe we haven't understood Spinoza so well after all.

Let it be given then that the world is the set of the best possible images, and also of the best images possible. On the surface, inflection is the mark of images that can't be the best, and that are thus outside the world and its inclines, though they are a part of it. Take any surface. Generally, we describe its relief in terms of summits and crests, basins and valleys. But if we can manage to erase our coordinate axes, then we will only see inflections, or other intrinsic singularities that describe the surface precisely. They are the sign that the best possible are not given, and that the possible best are not even called forth. Nothing is lacking in the definition of these points of inflection; they simply signify a suspension of world.

When, in the images that surround us, we are able to concentrate only on inflections, we accede to another regime of images that we will call primary ones. This perception is necessarily fleeting and variable, since we can't become "used" to it. We can't settle into it through the determination of a best reaction; it is a

mobile image in which an unlocatable position eludes our comfort. Primary in this case does not mean a first stage to which another would be added in order to create a better perception. No approximation is possible either: the primary image is right or it isn't. For any progressive sequence would make us lose these images that abide no support, no weighing down. They allow us to glimpse a pure temporality to which we can't accede as subjects. For that temporality is unlike Kantian interiority; it is the opposite, or worse than that. If indeed we stick to Kantian concepts, time, as a form of interiority, is contrasted with space, which is a form of exteriority. However, it may be possible for us to imagine a radical exteriority that would not be the opposite of an interiority.

Objects such as the Moebius strip, for example, cannot be understood when the inside/outside opposition is dramatized in this way. The interest of this sort of figure lies rather in the fact that it offers us a set of images in which inside and outside are notions devoid of meaning. Perhaps it is the virtue of such paradoxes, whether spatial or logical, to allow us to see, if only for an instant, a universe with no top or bottom, right or left, inside or outside (i.e., what we have been calling the set of primary images). Inflection would seem to be the constitutive element of such a paradox. The intersection of signs of concavity that this sign induces on either side of the curve would seem to be the equivalent of, or a planar projection of, the spatial paradox of the Moebius strip. This paradoxical sign would then give us a pure temporality: a form that would be prior to any interiority or exteriority. It would be the form of an absolute exteriority that is not even the exteriority of any given interiority, but which arises from that most interior place that can barely be perceived or even conceived, which is to say, in the paradoxical mode, that of which the perceiving itself is radically temporal or transitory: the nonsummable, the noncapitalizable.

We may now be able to further our understanding of the figures of baroque stylistics. The slippage we had noted at the site of the point of inflection in many baroque motifs would seek to expose this singularity. The whole question would then be to make the barely perceptible perceptible, without altering its nature. This eliminates any vectorial designation that would introduce a heaviness on that which can't bear being weighed down. And also, because of its essentially nonsummable and temporal character, it would not be wise to lengthen this point and turn it into a segment—in short, to make it last and to have us settle into our perception of it.

A first solution of the baroque was to flatten the curve, to ovalize it, in order to dislodge the point of singularity and place it in a zone of indiscernibility; hence the inversion of curvature was differed without being repeated. But whatever its merits, this process conforms all too well to the false notion that the baroque is a vague, imprecise style. On the contrary, orthogonal slippage must be seen as a process that specifies as precisely as possible, without vectorizing or emphasizing. This slippage must be read as a leap into another dimension, or rather, into another register of images. It would mark the access to a strange domain of the physics of matter, where the latter would offer no resistance to expansion. It is an indeterminate zone, in which action is no longer followed by reaction, as in the peculiar behavior of a piece of rubber stretched beyond its normal usage but before it breaks. It is a field of experience outside of the ordinary, where things are no longer resolved in terms of a minimizing of tension. It represents a departure from hodological space, but it is also another form of temporality: first, it is the passage from elastic reversibility to plastic irreversibility, but beyond that, and more surprisingly, it is a form of temporality that is not an expansion nor even a flow, for its fundamental characteristic is that it is not in phase.

"To be late," says the Greek *usterein*. *Hysteresis* is a gap in the time of the world through which we perceive pure instantaneity. It is the time of a universal lapping of waves that cannot be represented by a straight line or even a swirl, but only by a surface of variable curvature that is perpetually out of phase. It is the time that we perceive beneath the precariousness of things. It is that fragility of configurations in a state of hysteresis, while any expansion stretches out form and any return releases it; it is thus when any configuration escapes precariousness only in its transition toward a form that is always further expanded. Strictly speaking, the ungraspable is not the obscure or the informal but that which, in the full light of day, can be apprehended only as it is transformed.

We say that time flows, but then we also place ourselves in a landscape where valleys are burrowed and heights erected. Geography itself, that science of the nudity of surfaces, believed that it found its unity or its fundamental object in the hydrographic basin. Yet this space has only an extrinsic definition: delimited by a crest line and centered on the so-called line of greatest slope that is the thalweg. When we think of time in terms of flow, we are already funneling it into a gullet. And the abstract line that serves as the representation of the temporal coordinate is worth what the rectification of our waterways is worth: a gully space. In choosing this sort of object, geographers dug the ground out from under their feet, and, as they went deeper, they turned into geologists, or hydrographers, or many other things. The important thing henceforth was to distribute geographical space between specialties that were more or less physical or human. In short, they ceased being geographers, whereas, following the various fates of other scientific disciplines, other experts in turn did become so. Thus physicists, who have recently been following developments in microscopy, are now measuring the surface of the atoms of crystals without there ever being a question of drawing temporal lines.

And yet, simply as a matter of form, it already seemed clear that the hydrographic basin was not a good primary element, that it would never be the atom of surfaces. In section, a basin offers a gratuitous symmetry: a redundancy of apexes on either side of the longitudinal plane of the valley. Which is like defining the diameter of the circle as twice the radius. But if we erase one mountain, an inflection remains. Some will say: inflection isn't primary, for it comprises a punctual symmetry, precisely with respect to the point of inflection. But to say that is to ignore the difference between concavity and convexity. The important thing is that whatever their orientation in space might be, the two branches of an inflection will not have the same destiny, because

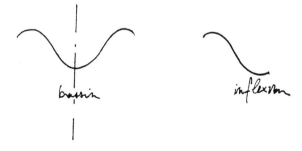

their curvatures are inverted. That is why inflection is the true atom of form, the true object of geography. Just a hill and a valley and nothing more allow for all possible becomings. Space is thus no longer a juxtaposition of basins but a surface of variable curvature. We will no longer say that time flows, but that time varies. No settling is possible in such a landscape: variable curvature turns us into nomads.

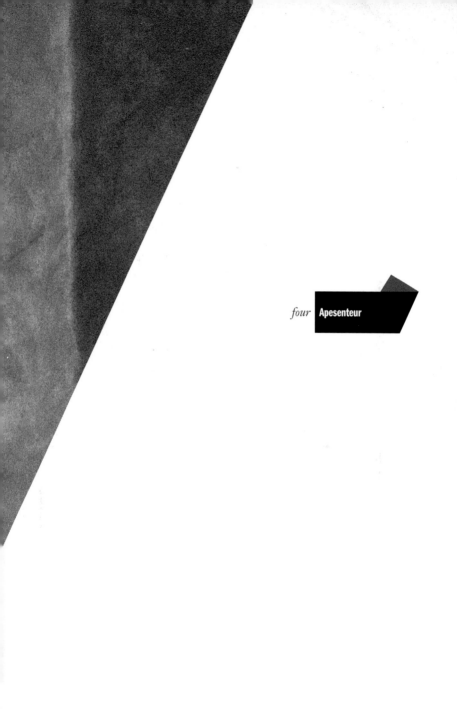

four **Apesenteur**

A table is made up of two dark wooden boards. We perceive its thickness through a slit afforded by a strip of glass. Both boards are supported by two different types of legs: the first is made of plywood and looks like a free surface that is nonetheless strictly defined: it is a ripple formed by the intensification of an inflection. Barely perceptible at ground level, this inflection deepens as it rises below the two boards. The shape of this leg is obtained by rubbing down a rough piece of plywood; that is how the colored lines of the different layers of wood that make up this manufactured material become exposed. The second leg connects both boards thanks to a metallic arc, which is itself supported by a stem. This stem ends in a cone that rests on its head.

Both legs are translated into the surface of the table. The ripple translates into a calligraphic sign made of bronze, while four mother-of-pearl disks point to the assembling of the metallic arc with the boards.

All landscapes can be described as hills and valleys, and time is said to flow. But geographically speaking, hills and valleys are maxima and minima whose definition presupposes the choice of a gravitational vector. Such that the reading of a landscape, in relation not to extrema but to inflections, leads us toward an experience of weightlessness.

This experience of weightlessness was aesthetic before it became technological. In his essay "Renaissance and Baroque," Wölfflin explains the baroque universe as having to do with a *gravitas*. This affect is as corporeal as it is spiritual: the heaviness of limbs as well as the preoccupations of the mind. More precisely, Wölfflin detects two elements in baroque experience: on one hand, the heavy consistency of the flesh, and on the other, the pathetic thrust of the subject who needs all his strength to resist crumbling under the

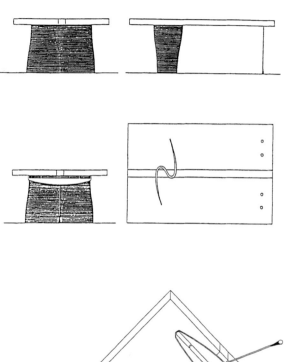

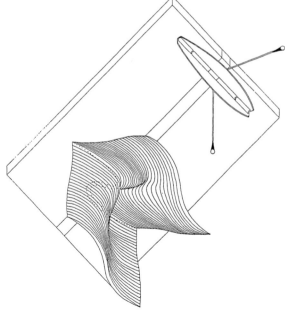

weight of his limbs: "The functioning of motor organs is deficient, the mind only masters the body imperfectly."

It is already difficult to know what people mean when they say "mind," but it is certainly even more difficult when it comes to "body." In Wölfflin's case, it might help if we go back to notions of elementary physics. Physics teaches us that the weight of a body is the product of two variables: mass and acceleration. Two elements thus come into play, namely the inertia of the body and the acceleration of gravity. We must then, in our everyday experience of the weight of things, define mass, whose effects vary according to a vector, which is gravity. As we have developed this habit through our long inhabitation of this planet, we have come to think of this gravity as an invariable. But what Wölfflin points out is precisely the variation of this gravitational vector that is due to an incongruence between muscular force and the inertia of the flesh.

It is as if, around 1630, a fundamental experience had emerged that had not yet found an adequate mode of inscription in science, ethics, or aesthetics. Descartes, who refers only to pure movement, speaks of a heavy substance that he says is all too dependent on corporeal substance. Inertia becomes evil, and force becomes a property of the mind. Later, in 1632, Galileo punctuates his reflections with the writing of his *Dialogues*, in which he says that beneath movement there is acceleration. And it is just at this time that Wölfflin, in agreement with Burkhardt, finds a change in baroque style, which, heavy and contrived at first, escapes little by little from its original gravity and gains in lightness and gaiety. It would almost seem as if the reflections of Galileo were followed by the aesthetic experiences of Michelangelo or Bernini. An entire gradation of gravity can be read into them, in the same way as the variation of a given parameter can be read in an experimental montage. The statues that encircle the facade of Saint Peter's could stand as a reference point: the true weight of things, the congruence of muscle and flesh. Thus we find, on either side of this equilibrium, the tombstone figures of the basilica of San Lorenzo that emphasize the weight of gravity, and inversely, the figures on the ceiling of Saint Ignatius whose mass dissolves into a floating inertia. The baroque age will then have exhibited this sort of vacillation in the possible connections between inertia and gravity.

But we must still clear up a misunderstanding. If we go back to the baroque experience today, it is not in the name of an eclecticism that would be the sign of our postmodern age. It is rather that our very contemporary experience gives this historical one an acute meaning, for we are now once again being exposed to variations of the gravitational vector. This is of course the consequence of explorations in space, of which one outcome is the reevaluation of chemical and biological processes under conditions of variable gravity: today in interstellar weightlessness, tomorrow probably in the hypergravity surrounding heavy planets. But in a more general way, variations in gravity are also relevant in all phenomena that are conceived in terms of fields of potentiality. Thus catastrophe theory is first of all a description of the deformation of extrinsic singularities in a field of potentiality whose surface continually bends before a given vector. But one could just as easily decide to immobilize the surface while varying the orientation of the vector. Thus it is for technological and scientific reasons that we are led back to the baroque experience. But soon these reasons will also be economic and sociological, for the industrial production of certain molecules in space is already under consideration.

We are of course not postulating any great unity between knowledge, technology, and society. It is no longer credible to us that beauty, practice, and the truth be said to coincide. Still, we are surprised at the way that modernism has been ostracized today in the name of a postmodernity whose eclecticism barely conceals its sterility. Yes, our epoch is characterized by its variety of lifestyles, by the rise of situations of hyperchoice; and how right we are to speak of a "floating space, without moorings or markers." Without gravity, we might say. Everything spreads out onto a single plane, without top or bottom, right or left. Modern optics speaks of this chiasmus where great causes have small effects and vice versa. But nonetheless, this plane has its own topography. On a continuum without values, everything can dissolve into inconsistency; however, if we negotiate its inflections, we can ensure continuities between the most disparate registers, between the most distant eras.

Each postulate of the modernist movement, once rid of the principle of unity, can be understood as the expression of a desire for continuity between the social, the technical, and the formal. For example, a flat roof is certainly not a building imperative—quite to the contrary.[3] Rather, it draws the asymptotic limit of the series of progressively less inclined roofs, and as such it might constitute the envelope of a free society to explore the range of its customary values. Instead of simply quoting inconsistent and gratuitous images, our epoch takes up the modern challenge of continuity. If collage appeared to be the paradigm of modernism, it is because it allowed our eye to seek out that invisible line that traces a continuity between images, fields of knowledge, and the most diverse practices.

It seems that inflection is precisely the new sign of the modern continuum. It is an abstract and luminous sign that points to a world outside of gravity and its vectors. All too often, abstraction is reduced to a few circumscribed geometrical figures expressing relations of equality or commensurability. These are, primarily, the circle, the square, and the equilateral triangle. In fact, in most commentaries on avant-garde works of the beginning of the century, many other formal elements were indeed overlooked, even though artists sought in them a way of the future. As Klee would say: "The freedom of the stroke does not easily submit to the final effect one wishes to realize; an activity develops which, out of prudence, only still uses a restricted number of lines. We are still at a primitive stage."

In the same way, Le Corbusier's statement of the five elements of modern architecture culminates in the free plan that allows the inflections of variable curvature to emerge. It is as if modern artists had been moving toward this sign about which they still weren't sure. For inflection was something that both escaped crystalline geometry and heralded a new geometry as yet unknown. Those modernists also knew that they had, above all, to avoid two opposite pitfalls: a dissolution into the indefinite and a return to the representation of natural form. Thus on one hand the loss of form, and on the other the organicist maze into which art nouveau had fallen. And indeed, these two dangers do quickly threaten when dealing with inflected form. This being the case, it seems that the more one confronts the continuum, the more important it is to remain in touch with the most abstract experience possible, even if the meaning of "abstract" is not yet quite clear. Fortunately, it is possible for us to find the path toward a new form of abstraction in the recent scientific developments that deal with a return to the visibility of geometry. Catastrophe theory, for example, shows us how to classify the singularities

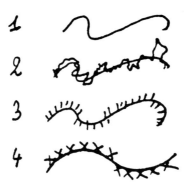

of surfaces with variable curvatures. First on fields of potentiality where one can distinguish crests, apexes, valleys, etc., then on internal spaces where the set of possibilities is reduced to seven basic singularities, from the pleat to the umbilical. And precisely we have seen that the pleat is a series of inflections that are increasingly pronounced. But it is lucky that artists do know how to work with abstraction and create for themselves the abstract categories of the future.

This was in fact the task that Paul Klee devoted himself to in his writings. In the first chapter of his course at the Bauhaus, we find this series of sketches entitled "active lines."

The first figure is a line of variable curvature, or a series of inflections. The second figure adds a second line to the first: variable curvature opens itself to chance. The third figure looks like a line covered with grass. The fourth figure repeats the third but in a more rigorous manner: there is only one element of inflection, and a distribution of the grass following the mathematical concept of concavity or radius of curvature.

We have seen that in and of itself, inflection referred to a weightless state of things, without top or bottom, right or left. This state of things lacks in nothing and only represents a certain mode of being of images. Klee's series of sketches shows us that inflection is at the crossroads of several paths: on one hand, variation in curvature opens itself to chance and inflection resolves itself in fluctuations. The broken line of his second figure demonstrates the randomness that determines the surface of variable curvature and dissolves form: little by little, the waves make their way to the surface. Shaped like a wave, inflection introduces the form of the vague.

On the other hand, variation of curvature becomes an accent and allows its radii of curvature to show. It is as if inflection exhibited a capacity for division or accentuation: from a simple line, we now come to a multiplicity of vectors of concavity. Each point of curvature is vectorized and manifests a tendency. Yet these vectors of concavity have nothing to do with the gravitational vector; they are always intrinsic, while the gravitational vector always intervenes as an element that is extrinsic to the definition of the curve.

Moreover, an essential property of variation of curvature is that it constantly sends off new radii toward a variable center; vectors of concavity thus always move as a cluster or multiplicity, whereas gravitational vectors obey a law of selection that gives them their quality of uniqueness. If the former are a feel, like velvet, the latter are a hold like a bite. And yet the first bring about the second. Gravitational vectors are unique only in being twofold. Actions seek resistance, vectors oppose vectors; therein lies their second nature. It is then necessary, if the vector is to be related to the curve, that inflection itself have a capacity for resistance. It is a strange kind of resistance, by itself and for itself; a primary resistance, prior even to the power struggle; it is a tendency that precedes the vector.

There are at least two painters who have known how to abstract these different categories of images. The first is Klee, of course, in whose work vectors can be found everywhere. Paintings like *Unstable Equilibrium* (1922) or *The Wind of Roses* of the same year demonstrate to what extent Klee was a master of the vectorial diagram. Equally remarkable is his research on the line of variable curvature. In *Snake Paths* (1934) the curvature of the snake is nothing other than a bifurcation of singularities on a surface of propagating waves; in *Berg und Luft* it becomes the surface of the outer limits of the atmosphere and of geography. But it is in his paintings that are very sparse in their composition that one perhaps finds the simplest and most moving vision of these different categories of images. *Incandescent Landscape* might be said to contain an entire philosophy of the image. The profile of the landscape is an inflection of which Klee wanted to emphasize only the most tenuous curvature. On the left, a cart holds up a set of points while others lie on the ground. This piling up and this dispersion are two signs of the opening of inflection to chance. It may be that these points are points of flection that are available for the creation of other free articulations, like the two points that rework the landscape's profile. Then, moving uphill, we find two elements that are the abstract signs of the two opposite tendencies of vegetable life: the first, dormitive, the second, germinative. And finally, on the right, there is the vector that is determined by an oblique gravitational axis. But what is the value of the solitary dot on the bottom right?

A second painter in whose work the vector is constantly present is one of our contemporaries: Francis Bacon. Painting leads Bacon from an experience of the body to an experience of the earth. That is why we don't find the abstract sign of inflection in his work but, in a very direct way, the surface of variable curvature. It is a visible directness when it occurs in abstract landscapes, but it is equally direct when it is that invisible perspective that disfigures faces: the mirror of variable curvature. Landscapes and faces bend like velvety surfaces under the hold of the vector. Tendency is exposed to the bite. Perhaps because of the problem of giving a colored expression to white skin, Bacon, as he worked on bodies, had to explore all pictorial possibilities: from the pearly to the grassy, from the sandlike to the velvety. *Sand Dune*. And as he surveyed these various states of the flesh, another experience necessarily arose: that of the rough, the brutal, or even the brutish. This can be seen in the imprint made by the abstract monochrome vector on the velvety skin of the landscape, but it could already be found in the concrete bite of the first paintings, such as *Crucifixion-1947*. Thus in Bacon's work, the surface of variable curvature does indeed withstand a tendency that allows it to be vectorized, but does this surface open itself up to chance?

Bacon works hard and isn't easily satisfied. For this among other reasons he sees the gratuitousness that cuts through all things. Thus extreme precision encounters chance, and a splash of paint hits the surface of variable curvature like a wave. Or else, in a quieter mode, inflection inserts itself into the fractal passage from the pearly to the velvety. A true in-between, inflection is that equilibrium between chance and tendency, where the sandlike and the pearly are on the side of chance, and the velvety and the grasslike on the side of tendency.

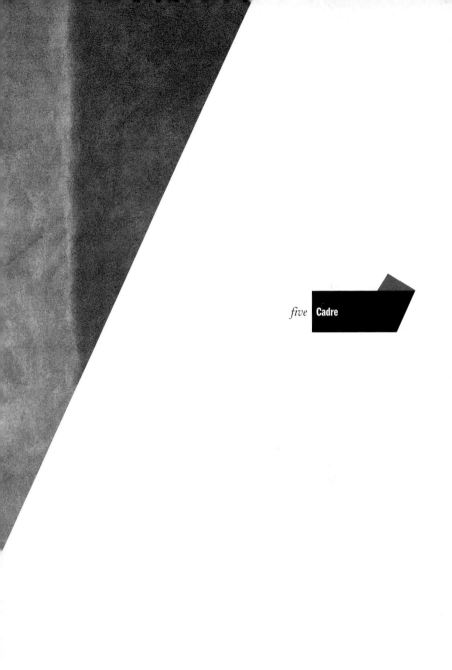

five **Cadre**

A writing desk and its armchair are made of plywood. The two objects are linked by a series of mortise and tenon joints. Together they form a single trapezoidal object, for the upper part of this unit assembles in a continuous surface the back of the armchair, the armrests, and the shelves that frame the working area of the study. A potential user would thus be totally enclosed in this space. Tracks on the ground would help that same user set the armchair against a wall.

We are postulating that the objects that surround us can be perceived from a purely formal point of view, independently of their concrete purpose. Territories, buildings, and objects present their own particular visibilities, which allows us to classify them into categories of images. We have seen that territories, in their specificity, are inflection images. We will see that objects are primarily vector images, but first we will choose to call "architectural" everything that is a *frame*. This does not preclude a certain mixing of genres, where a piece can be furniture only in its purpose, while being architecture or geography in its form. The most important thing is that we discern the formal characteristics of the images we are dealing with.

Inflection is that image which resolves itself in fluctuations while emitting its radii of curvature as so many tendencies. Facing inflection, the vector presents its four constitutive parts: direction, orientation, length, and point of application. What are then the formal characteristics of the frame image? The three abstract functions of the frame presuppose a form that is independent of its content. An interval separates the order of causes from that of effects. But the more a frame shows itself to be independent from its content or its function, the more one must bring out the principles of its formal autonomy.

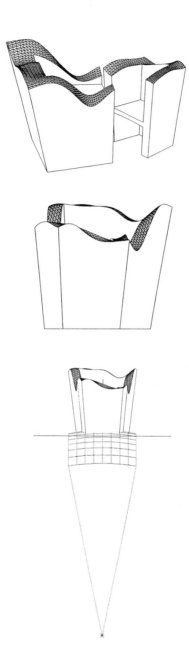

Let us assume that we have to build a simple frame such as the frame of a square painting. We can proceed in two ways. The simplest is to assemble four pieces of wood of equal length. A distortable quadrilateral is then produced that can be stabilized by fixing two braces along the diagonals. The second way of building this frame requires greater skill, for instead of fixing braces, one must assemble a jointing that fits with at least one of the articulations of the frame; in this way, it will seem stable in itself. In each construct, we can see that two principles are involved: the equal length of the pieces of wood and the stability of their assembly.

The first principle is one of geometrical legality. The register of framing shapes consists of three fundamental forms: the circle, the square, and the equilateral triangle. These forms obey the principle according to which equality is the same as legality. Thus even in the most complex frames, we will be able to find at least one principle of symmetry that defines the equality of two of the parts. And if by chance a frame is not symmetrical, it is because it has undergone operations of an adjunctive or subtractive type. Certain frames can become distorted, as when the square slopes toward the lozenge, but this is an artifice that only serves to demonstrate more clearly the second principle of the frame: its stability. It is our eye that must then reestablish the balance of the composition.

Let us now return to the abstract functions of the frame. The frame selects a vector from among a multiplicity of possibilities, but no principle of optimization is yet involved. Indeed, a comparison among vectors supposes an applicability of vectors on each other that is not given in advance; vector to vector relations create action systems that are never simple. For action is in itself complex, as the vector is inseparable from a clinamen.

The reaction, in turn, becomes doubly complex, for it always includes a tendency to evade. The opposability of forces that allows us to rank them from the greatest to the weakest thus depends on the establishment of artificial conditions of stability, of coupling, of diagonalization, or of feedback that regulate the field of free forces before they can confront one another or be measured.

We normally think it is gravity that makes us stand upright, and we therefore forget that it is diagonalization that prevents us from falling down. As if we were nothing but a weight. But our everyday actions and reactions take place within frames of support that prevent any evasion. C. S. Peirce's philosophy is very enlightening in this regard and is in fact most exciting. Ever since Newton, philosophy has dealt with a concept of force that is viewed as a type of law. The fact that apples fall is a matter of legality, and whoever doesn't subscribe to this view is suspected of substantialism. One of the great merits of Peirce's philosophy is that it does not confuse the experience of force with the legality of gravitation. Yet Peirce cannot be accused of being a substantialist; he simply persists in maintaining that our everyday experience of force is at least threefold: tendency, effort, and legality. It is not a question of looking for something lurking behind a curtain, but of finding something that is on that curtain and on its very folds; something that a poorly understood science has kept hidden. Newton's gravity does not represent a progress with respect to the conatus and the live forces of Spinoza and Leibniz; it is simply the disclosure of a third register of images of forces: the one that exposes experimental frames.

The frame selects because it eliminates the tendency for evasion. And what holds true in physics also holds true in society. A great tradition in anthropology has placed the gift at the origin of society, though Peirce is probably the one to have best defined its formal nature. The gift is a relation that always involves three terms. The fact that A gives B to C has nothing to do with the double fact that A parts with B and gains possession of C. The proof is that C can very easily refuse to appropriate B, but this will never eliminate the inescapable fact that A gave him B. Through this gift, C has entered into the aim of A, and whatever he does, it is within this framework that he will henceforth have to act. This sort of aim is the best example one can find of a ternary relation: within the optical frame of the gift, there is no escape possible, and the donor is involved as much as are the receiver or the gift itself.

Marcel Mauss was the first to have stressed the essential and persistent nature of the gift, which he saw as being at the origin of even the most primitive societies. It is not that the gift is the expression of any sort of sentiment; on the contrary, it produces a social bond that covers a great variety of affects, from generosity to aggressivity. Above all, Mauss had seen that one couldn't escape the gift, and that it created an obligation to give, to receive, and to give back again. But it was Lévi-Strauss who had the structuralist intuition. This triple obligation was really only one: the obligation to exchange. The gift has nothing to do with feelings, nor does it have a utilitarian function. One does not receive a gift in order to satisfy a need and thus to minimize stress, but to establish a relationship that places people and things within the frame of ternary images. Or rather that places our affects and our perceptions in the commensurable world of people and things. It is a world that is organized by the legality and stability of forms. The gift inscribes our actions within a frame that makes them stable and measurable, and thus establishes the equality of exchange as the law of circulation of words, goods, and women.

The architectural frame not only makes humanity probable, it also makes its structures visible. In his *Theory of Justice*, Rawls showed that the just frame of social exchange is determined by the same formal principles as the material frame. The first principle formulates an equality of rights, while the second principle establishes compensation in deeds. The form of juridical equality is coupled with a diagonalization according to which the economic privileges of some offer some advantages in return for the underprivileged others. By examining the different modalities of the frame in this way, we will be able to determine the relative visibility of the principle of equality and of stability.

First of all, let us take the frames that express primarily the law of equality. They are the regular geometrical figures: the circle, the square, and the equilateral triangle, followed by the set of regular polygons. In this register of forms, equality is first and stability second. The sides are obviously equal, while the stability of this relation of equality introduces a range of secondary elements that include ropes, tie rods, diagonals, St. Andrew's crosses, etc. These are the entire set of regulating figures that, from the Greeks to Le Corbusier, make the elements of equality or of symmetry commensurable and stable. In this respect, the equilateral triangle occupies a remarkable place in the series of regular polygons with n sides. For when the number of sides grows to infinity, we arrive at the circle, which is the maximal polygon; but conversely, when the number of sides decreases, we find the three-sided equilateral triangle. Not only is this triangle the minimal polygon, it is also the figure whose diagonals are identical to its sides, where thus legality and stability coincide. And it is perhaps the formal coincidence of these two principles of the frame that explains the fascination that this figure has exerted on many an architect.

In the second place, we will find the register of forms that relate to the construction techniques of the frame, whether they be made of wood or of stone. It is as if, in this register, legality had become secondary, allowing only stability to transpire. The first form in this register is the trapezoid that is found in tenon and mortise jointings as well as in buttresses and keystones. Unlike tie rods or diagonals, this formal vocabulary of stability is seldom realized. The trapezoid is an implied form of stability; that is why little attention has been paid to it other than in technical works. Thus trapezoidal forms are only perceived as a composition or degeneration of simpler forms: squares and triangles. The trapezoid is not considered a form in itself because no attention is paid to the scheme of action and reaction whereby wedging neutralizes the possibility of evasion through slippage. In the same way, another implied form of stability is ignored: the notch, which is the opposite of evasion through rotation. In this case, the concrete figures become the arc or the notched circle. From carpentry and masonry, we move on to mechanics; the frame becomes temporal and we encounter legality once again in the form of the notched circle that is the spatial sign of a periodization.

If we follow this double movement in this way, the entire range of framing forms can be described. First, we start with the circle and its infinite number of diameters, and end with the triangle whose diagonals are identical to its sides. This is the series of forms where legality predominates. But as soon as the diagonals of a triangle are fused with its sides, the apexes

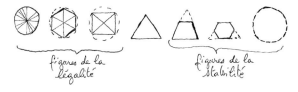

loose their importance, and through the elision of one of them, we get the trapezoid. Egyptian architecture demonstrates this procedure: in Luxor, the portico of the temple is a truncated pyramid, while the apex is erected into an obelisk. We then reverse the movement, find again the series of polygons through the successive truncating of the apexes, and end up with the notched circle. These are the framing forms where stability predominates. From the cosmic legality of celestial spheres to the stability of solar repetition, we are in fact listing the series of the primitive frames of thought. These are frames from which we cannot escape, unless we find our way into other categories of images.

In the same manner, the writing desk, which is the object of this chapter, exteriorizes the implicit form of the trapezoid and interiorizes the frame outlined by the working space: cabinetry of the trapezoid, architecture of the square, geography of the surface of variable curvature. The frame sinks into the ground. The figure of the tomb has often haunted the minds of architects. Adolf Loos, who always placed more importance on facing than on structure, saw in the tumulus the archetype of architecture as art. This is because the pyramidal shape of the tumulus is the natural outcome of the tomb being covered with the earth that accumulates on top of it. But we must dig out before we cover up. The first architectural gesture is acted upon the earth: it is our grave or our foundation. A plane against a surface of variable curvature, the first frame is an excavation. But perhaps this is just the bedrock of western thought. We put substance first: the hard, the full. Eastern thought puts the void first, and therefore the first frame is not an excavation but its negative: a screen. Unlike our western architecture whose first frame confronts the earth, Japanese architecture raises its screens to the wind, the light, and the rain. Partitions and parasols rather than excavations: screens emphasize the void.

The displacement of the categories of western thought from substance to image that we are witnessing today offers perhaps the conditions of a possible encounter with an East that is itself tending toward change. Bergson's concept of the image seems to allow for a convergence between a philosophy of the full—"All images are something"—with a philosophy of the void—"Everything is only an image." The concept of image combines an exigency of the full with that of universal variation: "All images constantly interact with all others." In this full light of continual variation, the void inserts itself like a dark spot raised by the screen of our consciousness; it is a moment of indeterminacy in the interactions of light.

The framing of emptiness within the fullness of light defines the screen. It is a leitmotiv of Francis

Bacon's painting. Sometimes it takes the form of walls or tiles suspended in space, at others this architecture of primary screens culminates in the unfolding of umbrellas. But the crucial moment occurs in the passage from the framing of the full color of the background to the empty screen of a dawning of consciousness: a *painting*? It is neither frame nor screen, but a passage from the screen to the frame; it is the architecture of the cinematographical mechanism that has become so crucial in our times.

six **Dehors**

The front of this bookcase is striated with horizontal openings that give access to the books on the shelves. On the vertical, two beams hold the bookcase up against the wall. In the middle, a sheet of Plexiglas draws a colored line that contrasts with the natural finish of the wood. The strata of the plywood surface are sanded down in such a way as to reveal a relief of corresponding contour lines. The entire surface is then polished according to the traditional techniques of cabinetmaking.

Vittorio Gregotti advises architects to begin their work on a geographical scale. This, he says, is in order to bring out the specificity of the site and to ensure that the built frame institutes a network of rational connections that structure or modify the "shape of the territory." In short, it is to provide a project for the site. But there is at least a second reason why architects should deal with geography. Beyond the built frame there is the site, but beyond that still, there is the outside.

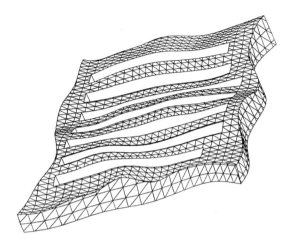

Geography is not the surroundings of the building, but rather the impossibility of its closure. But it is not a context either, for architectural punctuation is never final. We will therefore not speak of geography as a superior scale to the built frame, but rather as a principle of rupture of scale. And in this way, there will be no object, no matter how small, that does not have its geographical component.

Geography is not the field next door, nor even the neighboring district, but a line that passes through our objects, from the city to the teaspoon, along which there exists an absolute outside. This outside is not relative to a given inside; it exceeds any attempt at interiority. If there has been talk of a cinematographic device in architecture that allows for the passage from the frame to the screen, it is in part because architecture comprises a register of out-of-field images that is specific to it: the geographical image. Just as in rhetoric, where punctuation can be used in the name of silence rather than meaning, so the built frame can allow us to hear the geography that runs outside it, silently.

We start with the idea that geography offers us the shape of the outside. This must first be understood in a most straightforward way. The surface of the earth is indeed what we find outside buildings and what resists, for a while at least, human enclosure. But this can be better understood if we pay attention to the language of mathematicians. For them, geographical surfaces have become the privileged models of fractal objects. Mandelbrot writes very beautifully: "Look at any fractal object; if its dimension is comprised between 1.1 and 1.5, then you will easily find a geographical object that resembles it." This purely formal perspective through which he sees geographical surfaces reveals their exact nature. Like inflections that open themselves to fluctuations, geographical surfaces comprise an aleatory element whereby any interval can become the site of another complication. It is therefore not only the power of continuity that allows a virtual infinity to emerge between two points, contiguous as they may be. It is that between any points there is an interval, a zone of indeterminacy or availability that can always give rise, in an aleatory manner, to another fold. In this unruly geography, there is always time: time to take a detour and to leave the short-cut behind. What is near becomes distant for me, and geography fits into my—Japanese—garden.

Thus if we draw surfaces with variable curvatures within an architectural framework, we can say that we are introducing an outside on the inside; it is a furnishing in the sense that furniture is a property of the earth. The shape of an object like the bookcase, for instance, is not applied like a mold on clay, for the relief of this piece of furniture is constituted by the rise of the formal powers of its materials. As it is being sanded down, the different strata of wood dilate and appear as so many instances of detour and fold.

Then, inevitably, the fold falls away from the supporting structure and hangs like an oversized piece of clothing. Two architectural principles thus confront one another: the principle of structure and that of the skin. Modern architecture could be described as the site of confrontation between these two principles. Gropius or Le Corbusier, for example, invoked the primacy of structure over the skin as they concentrated on the scheme of pillars and allowed the facade to hang like an envelope. This would be the fifth element of modern architecture: the free facade. On the other hand, Adolf Loos (in *Spoken into the Void*), following Semper, called for the primacy of the skin that was "more ancient than construction." "First, there was clothing." The structural frame merely provides man with a cover as he takes off his clothes when he goes home: architecture becomes a clothes-hanger. The facade can then appear in its strictest structural truth, provided that the architecture is subordinated to the arrangement of the interior. While the outside walls are entirely disrobed, the walls of the rooms are lined with rugs, wood panels, or any other covering.

The surface of variable curvature thus leads us across the frame: from the geography outside to the furnishings inside. But we remain outside. From the shape on the outside that is geography, we have moved toward the shape of the outside that the folds of the facing espouse. It is as if architecture functioned as a topological operator: a frame crossed through by a Moebius strip. Passing over to the inside of the frame only sends us back to the outside of the strip.

But the description of a Moebius strip presupposes that one goes around it twice: once from the outside toward the inside, then a second time from the inside toward the outside. The fold took us from geography to facing; we must now return to geography through stripping. For covering up is also a baring. Modern beings become ever more naked as their walls with their cover-

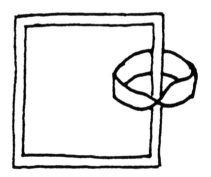

ings provide them with a protective sheath. Biological evolution might start to look like a protracted striptease. Michel Serres recently remarked that life has evolved from animal forms, where what is soft lies on the inside and is covered by a hard outside, to other forms, such as ours, where what is hard becomes interior: bones, cartilage, skeleton, while the soft is pressed out: flesh, mucous, skin. If we were to further this line of thought, we might wonder whether, by the end of this evolution, we might drop the bones altogether, then the flesh, then the epidermis. Only the dermis would remain. Not that we would be rid of the skeleton and the flesh altogether, but the skin would combine with them in new ways. The carapace having become bones would become a frame on which the flesh would spread the dermis. Rather than a disease, man would become the skin of the earth.[4] The modern body would become ever more vulnerable as it peals off its skin: Nietzsche was right to fear a disease. But perhaps he was also right to wish for it. In its modern constitution, the skin is no longer the sheath that protects the muscles, the viscera, and the skeleton; it is the latter that provide an echo chamber for the surface effects. Dermic power rises: the becoming of man-as-skin.

From geography to facing, and from dermis to earth, we are reviewing those primary images whose sign is inflection. We are speaking of a certain state of the earth and of the skin that is not their rudimentary state of being. The function of architectural facing is to make the dermis rise from under the epidermis, and to bring the skin to a surface condition that life will continually harden. Virtuality lies beneath the squama: it is a surface of resonance or a field of potentiality. For one cannot simply transfer the forms of the geographical outside onto furniture in order to get the outside inside. Earth and skin have to go through the trials of slough: skin stripped inside a padded room, but also the earth made bare, weightless, out-of-frame: the world given over to inflection.

All of evolution could be rethought in this way. Leroi-Gourhan had already remarked that mobility is an imperfect way of opposing the animal kingdom and the vegetable one. For alongside the species that are properly mobile, a bifurcation has allowed for the development of a number of invertebrate beings, sponges and other coelenterates; these are animals for whom locomotion plays no role at all and whose organization corresponds to the radial system of many plants. But the animal branch to which man belongs is organized according to movement, and the parts of the body line up on either side of a bilateral axis of symmetry that is oriented in a forward direction. Yet a return to immobility, the abandonment of movement, would be for us, vectorial animals, a conceivable option, and one might wonder whether the originality of man does not reside in that.

For our liberation from the requirements of locomotion does not lead us back to a radial organization; once our hands are freed, our body straightens up. In their superiority, humans would adopt an erect position and would proudly raise their spine against the gravitational vector. They would thus have remained vectorial, and evolution would simply be a permutation of axes, from the vector of movement to the vector of gravity.

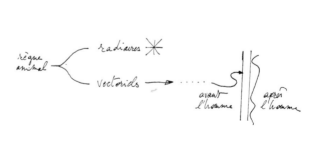

Basically, nothing new, other than an orthogonality of movement. But perhaps the advent of man represents more than a simple permutation; its impact would result from the abandonment of a vectorial status in favor of a spreading out on the surface. The becoming-of-man would consist in his coming upon an abstract frontal plane, of which our upright position would only be a consequence. With man, animality projects itself against a plane that is orthogonal to movement. Hence the importance of the great pictorial theme of the crucifixion. Ecce homo. The painting reconstructs the frontal plane on which the animal has projected itself. Cimabue, like many other primitives, made of the cross the system of generative axes of a plane; that is why Bacon was so interested in him. For once the frontal plane is in place, the projected flesh spreads out, slips and bends like a surface of variable curvature on an abstract plane: the fluctuations of the flesh become the play of dermic forces.

seven **Histoire**

The shell of this armchair made of plywood is composed of a series of vaults. The different layers of wood exhibit lines that are similar to the flow lines of a fluid along the fuselage of a projectile.

Inflection is a sign that describes surfaces of variable curvature. But these surfaces, between consistency and transistance, could just as easily be designated by other signs; thus the vault and the spiral are also possible figures of variation in curvature. Inflection, however, is that elementary sign that makes the center of curvature change sides on either side of the line or the surface. That is why inflection can be said to be the first abstract sign. Leroi-Gourhan had pointed this out in reference to prehistoric frescos. A spine was an abstract element that could bifurcate toward any animal: starting with a simple inflection, one could just as easily draw a reindeer or a bison. What then does the word "abstract" mean? In particular, if we maintain that inflection is an abstract sign, we must reconsider Worringer's notion that abstraction is characterized by crystalline geometry. Indeed, for him, inflection was the very opposite of abstraction, as it was the sign of the inverse of the will to art: *Einfühlung*.

Worringer had tried to divide the history of art into two great "wills." The term "will," certainly an idealist one, was in itself polemical. Going against the materialism of people like Semper, Worringer maintained that artistic forms were not determined by materials or techniques, but that they rather expressed the attitude of a given period toward life. Thus geometrical forms would have expressed the will to abstract art at a time of unease. At times when the outside world threatens, one would feel the need to withdraw from life and seek refuge in the contemplation of simple, crystalline

forms. At other times, artists would have taken pleasure in projecting their organic vitality into naturalistic forms. Rather than turning toward abstract geometry, these artists sensed a profound harmony between our instincts and the most disturbing aspects of life. At those times, vital inflection replaces crystals.

On one hand, then, a desire for abstraction and for retreat that was expressed most clearly in Egyptian art; on the other, an empathy with nature (*Einfühlung*) that was the basis of classical art. This being said, we are in no way diminishing the importance of Worringer's classification of forms, even if we are preserving his categories of images without paying too much attention to the different wills underlying them. We speak of primary images rather than of *Einfühlung*, and of tertiary images rather than of abstraction, to which we would add a category of secondary images.

Somewhere between the withdrawal of life into the abstraction of crystals and the participation in the shifting inflections of life, we might distinguish an intermediary attitude: neither withdrawal nor empathy, but confrontation. This would not be an added will to art, but an art of the will: a confrontation with life. Each vital attitude could then be recognized by a specific sign: inflection, vector, and frame. The three attitudes are not wills in the proper sense of a decision of a free and autonomous subject. They are rather three organizing systems between the subject and its territory or milieu; they have the quality of a power struggle. Toynbee classified civilizations according to their capacity for evolution or for self-transformation, and that capacity depended on the power relations that can transpire between a society and its milieu. Certain societies remain as if congealed because they are exhausted by their struggle with the environment: such is the case of Eskimo society withdrawn in its igloos. Other societies, on the other hand, stop evolving because nature has been generous to them and has satisfied all of their desires. Others, finally, evolve, because they take up the challenge of a milieu that neither satisfies nor crushes them. Hence withdrawal, empathy, and confrontation. However, Toynbee's thesis becomes uninteresting if the nature of this power is reduced to a simple calibration of forces facing each other, whether social or natural, that would allow us to determine the superior or the inferior one. Because these forces always produce all sorts of effects of resonance and evasion. But before any outcome, all measuring presupposes forces that seek one another. Ice banks and Eskimo sought one another and their blockage maybe comes from having found everything in each other. And a fortiori, the notions of organism and milieu are related in a way that is by no means natural: subject and milieu run after one another, must seek one another and find one another. One could go so far as to say that there is such a thing as a subject in an environment only when milieus seek one another and fold themselves onto an outside. Hence these three figures of the will or these three vital attitudes.

What then is the meaning of the term "abstract"? Abstraction would no longer characterize a particular will to art, but would designate a function of signs common to each of the three categories of images: the signs of a seizing of life. Indeed, to abstract means to take away, to isolate, to remove. Abstraction would be a sort of biopsy or geological section of life. In short, abstraction would be the end or the beginning of art as a sampling of life. Only the modalities of this sampling would vary according to the different vital attitudes. A bit in the manner of the Stoics, one should distinguish in abstraction all the nuances of the "cut." There would then be a firstness, a secondness, and a thirdness of the cut or section. The thirdness of the section would be the shape of the section itself, of the seizing effectuated upon things: the cubic, cylindrical, or other forms of the sampling—the planes of the crystal cleaved into things. The firstness would then refer to that which, on the abstract plane of the sampling, is not affected by the section, such as inflection, which persists in the section of a geographical relief. Finally, the secondness would be the event of the section itself. This would be the seizing itself and the sectioning that affects the surface of things, such as the edge of the dihedron or the point of the vector.

The form of the sample, the event of the seizing, and the portion of things that escapes this seizing would thus constitute the three modalities of abstraction that correspond to each of the three vital attitudes: withdrawal, confrontation, and empathy. It is obvious that art as sampling naturally suits one who withdraws from life and only wants to grasp it in bits and pieces. But it will also be practised for the mere violence and the sense of a hold upon things that this sort of act can inspire in us. Others, on the contrary, will seek in this sampling the sense we can have in life that things escape all possibility of capture, something like when an eel slithers out of the grasp of a fisherman's hand.

If abstraction is thus not a specific set of signs of a withdrawal from life, and corresponds rather to a practice of sampling that is basic to all artistic activity, we must also show, in an inverse manner, that the abstract art of the twentieth century has not been a monolithic phenomenon, and that its actual productions can be related to the three great attitudes that we have described. Thus Mondrian, Herbin, and Kandinsky are clearly the representatives of an abstraction that sticks to the contour of the sample, the limits of life. Hence the danger of this sort of painting, for it captures the quasi-frame of an interstitial life, just prior to crystalline death. Picasso, on the other hand, though he may have been called a cubist, was never interested in the cube and therefore not in quasi-crystals either. He was too instinctual, too powerful not to deal with life itself and assault it with form. That is why one seldom finds closed figures in his work: only dihedra or portions of cylinders that will instill some life into matter without really shutting it in. Form is merely a ruse through which the painter incites a force that is truly material. Each painting is like a move whereby Picasso exposes figures in order to find the lines or blocks of resistance in a mass that he then spurs with his brush. It is very revealing that Picasso is capable of treating a pregnant woman as a vector. There exists such a sculpture in the Paris Museum that shows that, far from being interested in pure form, Picasso was seeking the force that is contained in matter, the vector buried in the mass.

As for Klee, we have already mentioned his search for new abstract signs. They were those active lines along which life flees as one tries to capture it; lines not of resistance but of disappearance. It is in the strange nature of inflection that it changes qualities as soon as one tries to grasp it. Klee then carries Pollock to the moment where inflection turns into pure chance. It should be said that the genius of Japanese art was to have been able to develop an abstraction of the alea. It is a lyrical abstraction whose sign is the broken, fractal line. The section changes according to what is being sectioned, which in turn always escapes; but in this chase, it is hard to say what is escaping what, and whether, in the final count, the section line is what is most artificial or most natural, most abstract or most representational. When a Japanese painter or gardener draws a zigzagging footbridge, he looks for the aleatory fracture that cleaves all things and endows them with quality. Whether it be in the mane of imaginary lions, or the escarpment of cliffs, or the foaming of waves, they are the signs that Japanese art has been able to remain close to the primary undulations of life: where inflection is exposed to chance in such a way that tendency can emerge.

Following Worringer's advice, we should "train our eye to discern the different nuances of abstract art" as much as to inventory its signs. Twenty years after his *Abstraktion und Einfühlung,* Worringer questions the dual construction of his first book and tackles the problem of Gothic art. In the same way as did Byzantine art, Gothic art would constitute a stumbling block in his system that opposes abstraction and vitalism. The Gothic was all the more difficult to fit into his classification as he had tried to trace its evolution starting with its Nordic origins. Much before the architecture of its cathedrals, the Gothic will to art would have been expressed in the primitive masterpieces of northern ornamentation. It is there that we find the broken aleatory lines that, according to Worringer, attest to the presence of a strange nonorganic life in that they disregard the proportions of human or animal figures.

These lines are abstract and yet alive: "At each rupture, at each change in direction, we feel that forces that are suddenly arrested in their natural course straighten out and move on to the next movement with an intensity that has been increased by the obstacle. The more the ruptures are repeated and the more the line has obstacles to overcome, the more the undertow at the point of breakage is violent and the stronger the flow in the new direction; in other words, the stronger and the more driving the expression of the line."

Tendency peeps through from beneath the alea, and fluctuation takes on the form of an undertow. A new abstract sign appears: the singularity of the backup point. It is at that point that the return movement allows the tangential vector to emerge. In fact, the entire evolution of the Gothic is the history of the passage from one singularity to another: from the backup point to the vault. And if, according to Worringer, the northern Germanic soul was indeed the sine qua non of the Gothic, never would the beautiful constructions of the cathedrals have seen the light of day had this tempestuous soul not found a frame to temporize its movements. "Whether it was due to Roman law or to Christianity," the undertow had to go through an operation of symmetry so that simple tangency could become a vector in the form of a vault, as in the case of the rose window. In northern ornamentation, drapings and manes denatured the figures in such a way that the lines departed from any organicism and followed an autonomous course out of proportion with life. But the rose window offers a circular frame in which abstract lines are engaged: in the interlacing at the center of the circle, the backing-up turns into a vault. Gothic art is then that passage between two abstract signs: the backup point and the vault, whereby a tendency becomes a vector. It is the arrow of a spiritual thrust that transcends earthly existence and goes against its gravity to the point of dematerializing the bricks of its cathedrals. But it is also the sword that imposes the heavens on earth and subjects the serf to his master.

inflexion   ogive   rebroussement

ogive

rebroussement

Scanson gothique: ogive et rebroussement

eight **Subjectile/Objectile**

Computer-Assisted Conception and Fabrication (CFAO) systems have two types of use in industry. In mechanical engineering and building, pieces are designed that, though they can be complex, are in fact combinations of simple elements that can be drawn with a ruler and compass. Architecture can be reduced to a play of interlocking frames, and mechanical engineering deals with movements that are combinations of translation and rotation. The use of elementary primitives derives from this: segments of straight lines and arcs of circles. Furthermore, in automobile and aeronautical applications, the CFAO systems are also used to design casings; these are the contours of chassis or the wings of airplanes. The contours are not actually calculated but are subject to an adjustment procedure through wind tunnel tests. Also, their surface is drawn from approximated curves, Béziers or Splines, which are stretched on a bed of points positioned by hand. CFAO systems have certainly increased the productivity of the idea, but fundamentally they offer no advances over the work done by hand. Now, we can envisage second-generation systems in which objects are no longer designed but calculated. The use of parametric functions opens two great possibilities for us. First, this mode of conception allows complex forms to be designed that would be difficult to represent by traditional drawing methods. Instead of compositions of primitive or simple contours, we will have surfaces with variable curves and some volumes. Second, these second-generation systems lay the foundation for a nonstandard mode of production. In fact, the modification of calculation parameters allows the manufacture of a different shape for each object in the same series. Thus unique objects are produced industrially. We will call variable objects created from surfaces "subjectiles," and variable objects created from volumes "objectiles."

The question today is: what is an object? And this question only makes sense with respect to our daily objectivity, which is to say that set of things that industry conceives and fabricates and that we buy because they create use effects.

Pierre Clastres is responsible for explaining how the sexual identity of the Guaranis tribe is only suggested by biology. Following from this the adolescent must choose an object: a bow for men, a basket for women. A bow and basket are thus the figures of Guaranis sexual identity, just as vector and concavity form the figures of an extrinsic singularity in mathematics. And everything occurs as if we had found, in the house, the answer to what is happening on the outside. On the outside the vector indicated the site as an eminence in order to determine a territorial identity; on the inside the vector is this object opposite which one must position oneself to determine a sexual identity.

In every case identity shatters singularity. Maximum and minimum break the inflections of whatever curve; hills and valleys pass by in silence along the lines of the landscape, bow and basket assign the roles in sexual division, concavity and convexity oppose the object to the subjectile to determine a subject. And in every case a third element intervenes, because one does not determine oneself vis-à-vis the vector without passing through a frame. The extrinsic singularity presupposes the determination of a system of coordinates, territorial identity is only drawn within the frame of an architecture, the bow and the basket are adopted through the course of an initiation rite.

But it is clear that this objectivity has changed. It used to be that the object was simply what we saw in front of us; it was generally contrasted with the variations that are thought to take place within the subject. It

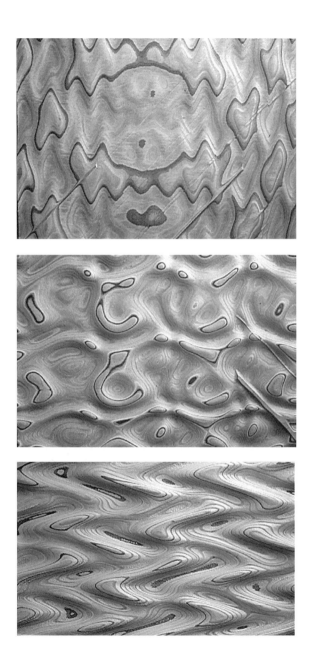

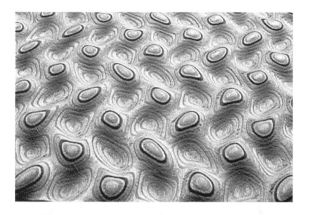

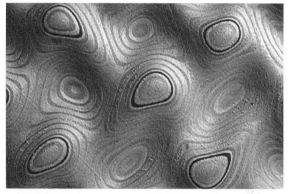

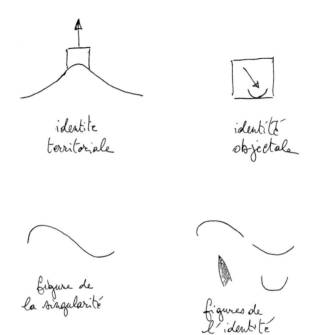

identité
territoriale

identité
objectale

figure de
la singularité

figures de
l'identité

was inseparable from a sense of clash or constraint that went together with a will to last or to resist. The object was thus first a vectorial image: a blade or a stick. It was a secondary image that was conceived in such a way as to maximize the exercise of a given force against its reaction. Whether it took the form of a knife, a vase, or a table, we always remained within vectorial singularities. An ogive, a basin, or a plane of orthogonality are still singularities with respect to the exercise of a vector. In this sense, the modernist movement has only accentuated this mode of objectivity. For it wished to eliminate everything that didn't contribute directly to usage or function and to build using a minimum of materials: it was a whole aesthetic of the engineer, by maximization. *Existenzminimum*. That is why ballistic contraptions such as rockets, missiles, and locomotives, all of which are eminently vectorial, still remain the archetype of object design.

But people forget that the vector image is subordinated to a frame image without which the vector only remains a tendency. Functionalism presupposes a certain kind of structuralism. For objects exist only inasmuch as there exists a sort of contract about their use or production. In the days of craftsmanship, the traditional object was overlain with a whole set of customs and usages that were the true source of objectivity, even if some objects only had the status of tertiary images: frame objects, fetishes, or symbols. These images did not exist in virtue of the contract; they were the very representation of it. In fact, an entire side of traditional decorative culture only served as a reminder of the contract that was at the origin of the object.

Conversely, at the time of technical reproducibility the object could assume an appearance of pure objectivity, as the repetition of the model was given as the only legality of the series. That is because the industrial norm first appeared as a simple law of constancy that had replaced the traditional contract. And when the norm took this form of a unique standard model, any legality other than that of repetition was a breach in the law of the series, to the point where ornamentation became something of a crime. The object was meant to maximize the utilitarian function, and its very repetition was the sign of its legality. Many also took this legality to be a form of equality: the identical object, produced by the masses for the masses. But this sort of contract is no longer viable today. For the standard model is not the same as equality and the norm is not the same as the law. Now that generations of industrial objects are constantly being replaced by new ones, we feel that the nature of the contract has changed, and hence also the nature of the object. Modern objects are eroded by time. The permanence of the law gives way to the fluctuation of the norm. The modern quasi-crystal is no more than a quasi-object. What is at stake is the convergence of a number of factors that influence each stage in the life of a product:

Consumption: our everyday actions invariably pass from the realm of tradition or law to that of the norm. The purpose of the norm is not to stabilize our movements; on the contrary, it is to amplify the fluctuations or aberrations in our behavior. Changes are the mode of the norm. The rigid elements of our behavior are articulated with one another in order to produce increasingly variable configurations. Objects, which are those solid parts of our actions, are but a moment of densification in the folds of our behavior that is itself fluctuating. The object has become inconsistent, a gadget that is replaced by other gadgets; but it can also become the singular nodal point of a modern continuum through variation. We are then faced with a new category of images: no longer vectors and their opposite reactions, but inflections that our behavior exposes.

Production: digital machines and productive technologies in general allow for the production of an industrial continuum. From the mold we move toward modulation. We no longer apply a preset form on inert matter, but lay out the parameters of a surface of variable curvature. A milling machine that is commanded numerically does not regulate itself according to the build of the machine; it rather describes the variable curvature of a surface of possibility. The image-machine organization is reversed:

the design of the object is no longer subordinated to mechanical geometry; it is the machine that is directly integrated into the technology of a synthesized image.

Representation: henceforth, the image takes precedence over the object. The CFAO image, malleable in real time, has lowered the status of the prototype, as well as all the representation of the object. The modes of production of images, as in the case of advertising images, are no longer derivatives of this primary one. One often hears about the image of a product, but in fact the product itself is in the first place an image. For simulation produces simulacra at the same time as the model changes its meaning.

Modeling: the primary image is no longer the image of the object but the image of the set of constraints at the intersection of which the object is created. This object no longer reproduces a model of imitation, but actualizes a model of simulation. The anatomical gestures of the user, the surface of the set of constraints of the material, the curves of optimization and of management, all constitute the geography that governs the object. Through television sales, the factory and its flexible workshops become the utopian site of the ideal market. The object, as well as the fluctuations in its price, is modulated at the intersection of the curves of supply and demand.

Function: a field of surfaces thus governs the object that has now become the set of possibilities of their intersection. But the surface of the object also becomes separated from its function when the latter is no longer mechanical but electronic. Just as Leibniz had conceived it, texts, information, images, and sounds are now all the object of numerical manipulation, so much so that the electronic parts that make up the functional core of the modern object no longer have anything to do with the visual or auditory restitution that realizes their concrete function. There are no more mechanical forces, only simple plates of integrated circuits that have but a determinable relation to the function of the object. The external shape of the modern object has only an aleatory relation with the electronic function. The shape of this new objectivity prolongs surfaces of resonance, whether screens or membranes, that restore the materiality of the numerical processes. Data of this sort can then create an image on a cathodic screen, but it can also create a sound on an acoustic membrane or, better still, produce a surface of variable curvature.

Marketing: an alea puts form in a state of fluctuation that offers us a true image of the norm. But it is no longer that standardized object that is defined by a law of repetition; rather it is this quasi-object that is but a fragment of a surface of possibilities where each exemplum is different. Yet it is not a personalized object, either, intended for a preidentified client. It is an object that fluctuates on the curve of variation of a new industrial series. It is an ordinary object that may well entertain singular relations with a user.

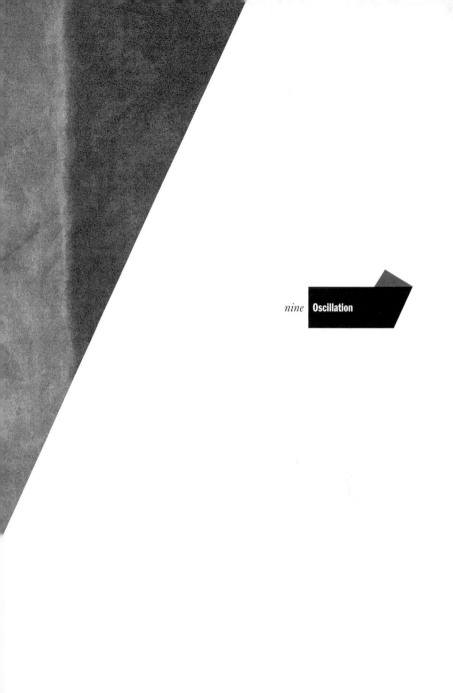

nine **Oscillation**

The surface of this table can be achieved by sanding down a rough piece of plywood. On one side, the board folds in as it offers its outer facing to two metallic legs. That extremity can be used for storing documents. The surface itself undergoes a slight variation in curvature, thus allowing its user to seek the inflection or the horizontal plane. The four legs are treated with nickel.

It is useful at this point to draw up an inventory of the various images that we have mentioned so far. The best thing might be to go back to Klee's sketches.

The fundamental image, the one we have been calling primary image, is inflection. Inflection is the sign of images that are strictly defined while being ungraspable. Indeed, we have seen that these images are precarious and fleeting since they are altered by existential factors and by their vectors. It is a case of either/or: either the primary image is capable of bearing a vector and offers a distribution of extrinsic singularities, maximum and minimum (in this case, vectors of concavity expose curvature as a cluster of tendencies), or, on the contrary, an inflection appears to bear no tendency at all, and its incurvation is resolved in simple, inconsistent fluctuation. In the second case, the vector captures nothing at all, as it is inapplicable to pure dispersion. Klee's sketches therefore raise the same question as does any primary image: will inflection turn out to be fluctuation or tendency?

First then, the primary image of inflection, because it presents itself as itself and by itself. Then, the secondary image of the vector, because on top of their orientation, direction, and module, all vectors have some sort of application as their aim. Vectors seek vectors, and endlessly build relations of an action-reaction sort. There again, two cases are possible, for these relations

can remain crude and amount to nothing but a series of evasions. As long as no frame is established in which the diagonals neutralize the possibility of deviation, the relation between one vector and another will remain a confrontation for its own sake, with no external purpose. The definition of a vector as something comparable and measurable presupposes the inclusion of a third element.

The nature of the frame is precisely ternary when the question of aim is taken into account, as is the case with the social frame that is constituted by the gift. The relation through which A has C as its aim as it gives it B is irreducibly ternary, in the sense that it does not con-

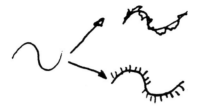

sist in two relations, between A and B on one hand and B and C on the other. The same goes for the architectural frame as it selects an orientation on the territory. It is in the nature of our Euclidian space to retain only ternary relations. Thus any two points lined up in space remain a virtuality as long as only these two points are being considered. But this lining up becomes an actualized relation as soon as a third point on this same line is selected. The ternary nature of the frame contradicts our habitual conception of it as being a square, and thus a quaternary relation. But if we look at the formal nature of the selective function, we see that the frame appears as a line of sight that defines the third point through which two points of a rudimentary alignment are definitely targeted, whatever the imprecision of their respective positions may be.

We then have our three fundamental images: inflections or primary images, vectors or secondary images, and frames or tertiary images. Two things must now be done. First, we must close our inventory with these three images, even if we end up inserting intermediary ones. For there is no point in going further if it is possible to recompose any image from a combination of our three elementary ones. For this, we rely on Peirce's demonstrations, and in particular on his abstract graph of spatial relations. You will never be able, he says, to recompose a graph of complex relations by juxtaposing binary elements and single elements, while all combinations become possible as soon as ternary relations are introduced. Peirce takes the example of a network of roads. One doesn't recompose a complex network by juxtaposing dead ends (one single extremity) and segments of roads (two free extremities), for in such a case one could only draw straight lines or loops. However, as soon as an element of bifurcation that comprises at least three branches is introduced, it becomes possible to recompose a network with complex intersections. There is therefore no point in trying to find elementary images beyond ternary ones.

It is also true that underlying the primary image, all sorts of images exist in a state of pure dispersion. They are the result of the interaction of images amongst themselves. They belong to the realm of aleatory images whose forms are never defined, because they are always recomposed according to the fate of their encounters. But as we are only interested in that which bears a form, we will leave this sort of interaction aside and will choose to call primary image any emergence of quality in such interactive contexts. Any chance occurrence or alea bearing a quality, and thus any fractal figure, will be considered an inflection of the fluctuating type.

Second, we must consider the consequences of closing our inventory. As soon as we claim that all images can be reduced to the smaller number of categories exposed above, we move from the question of image to that of visibility. For as long as we were only inventorying, images were juxtaposed to images according to their encounters; but now, we are closing this catalog and are claiming to encompass "all that is visible." The concept of visibility thus takes precedence over the concept of image. But a problem remains: what is the visibility of the image? For it doesn't seem right to reduce all of vision to three images, unless we ask what is visible *between* these images.

But to think about visibility is the very opposite of thinking about what is evident. Evidence is the flattening out of an image that puts an end to all discussion, whereas thought can only be renewed when one starts to think about what is visible in what seems evident. Vision passes between images as thought passes between concepts, which is why what is visible determines what is sayable and vice versa. Philosophy can therefore be said to be directly connected to the arts and should no longer pose as their censor nor as their commentator. As it leaves its channels of evidence, philosophy exposes surfaces of visibility where singularities lead to concepts.

Given these two propositions, we will turn to the major hypothesis developed by Simondon in his book *L'individu et sa genèse physico-biologique* (pp. 100ff.). According to Simondon, life would be inserted into matter in an indefinitely differed process of crystallization. Life is therefore not so much an accretion to matter as it is a sort of entrenchment. In order to prove his hypothesis, he explains in detail the formation of crystals, which he takes to be the absolute end of physical individuation. Any subsequent individuation would be prior to crystals, as these represent the terminal image of the process of mineral individuation.

The background picture against which a process of crystallization takes place is that of an supersaturated chemical solution. This solution appears as a potential field containing excess energy. The medium crystallizes when a germ is inserted into this potential field. The germ produces two effects: on one hand, the asymmetry of the germ destabilizes the energy contained in the solution; on the other, the germ gives this destabilized energy the frame of a structure that prefigures the crystal. Thus when a certain quantum of energy is picked up by this structure, a polarity is created in the potential field that engages the chemical solution in an unlimited process of crystallization. Simondon points out that the polarization of the medium is first a cause and then a consequence. The first polarization is that simple clinamen that destabilizes the medium and causes it to structure. The second form of polarity is then the result of the action of the crystal on the rest of the solution: it is a vector of growth.

Thus it would appear at first that Simondon only distinguishes between three types of image: the potential field of the initial solution, the germ that sets off the process of crystallization, and the structure of the crystal. But then one can see that each of these three images gives rise to further distinctions. First of all, the surface of the potential field comprises both the molecular alea of metastable energy and the autogerminative tendencies of the oversaturated solution. Then one must evaluate the consequences of the double nature of the vectorial polarization induced first by the germ and second by the structure of the crystal. Finally, a third level—that of the structure of individuation—must become the object of new distinctions, since the whole idea for Simondon is that life doesn't develop after crystals, but before them. The reason for this is that crystalline structures exhaust the potential energy of the medium, and thus the only possible developments are reproductions that are identical to crystals: their maximal growth. The whole trick of life then consists in suspending the process of crystallization by creating precrystalline structures that don't exhaust the medium's potential and allow its becoming to move on toward other individuations. Generically speaking, we would call "quasi-crystals" these structures whose meshing is looser than that of the crystalline networks.

FIG
Galaratese
A. Rossi

CADRE
DE
CONTRE VENTEMENT
(tableau)

FIG
Structure
métallique

QUASI CADRE
ARTICULÉ
(cerf volant)

   In the same way, our classification into three elementary images conceals a series of nuances that we must now explain if we are to fully understand these images. Underlying inflection, there is fluctuation. Between inflection and vector, there is the vector of concavity or tendency. And finally, we had mentioned the possibility for modern man of entertaining loose relations with the frame. This presupposes in turn that the structure of modern frames offers a certain amount of play. For just when the skin falls away from the structure and is no longer at one with it, the flesh serves as an intermediary that holds together this loose relation between the structure and the skin. In the modern frame, the function of diagonalization leaves the structure in order to be secured by the envelope it upholds. From the stability of the law, we have moved toward the tensions of the norm.

The frame is thus no longer an autonomous and predetermined form that imposes itself upon the canvas of the painting, whether as an equilateral triangle or as a diagonalized square; it is rather that the tensions of the surface now lend a relative stability to the articulation of the frame. The rigid parts of the frame still retain a certain geometry, but their articulation is mobile and their equilibrium results from the play of tensions that run through the system as a whole.[5]

The frame of a painting is no longer like a window, but rather like a kite: the tensions of the fabric stabilize the articulation of the intersecting pieces of wood. The square becomes a lozenge, and diagonals become the primary elements of the structure. But they are no longer simple tie rods that ensure the stability of the frame, they are its principal components. They establish principles of legality in this bendable quasi-frame whose tensions fold the fabric and allow its inflections to rise forth.

That is what happens to Mondrian's squares. In the first period of his work, the square is a window opened

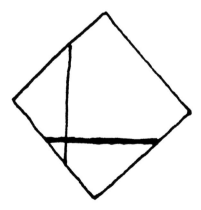

onto the future, but the painting is already no longer a perfect square, "only a quasi-square," as Michel Butor tells us. Besides, none of his paintings are symmetrical, as if Mondrian were seeking a certain freedom while nonetheless grappling with the most crystalline geometry. This search for the quasi-frame culminates in the famous painting of Hilversum, which he did for the Amsterdam museum in 1931. The square is a perfect one, but it undergoes a 45½-degree rotation and stands on one point. There is no more color; there are only two black lines parallel to the diagonals that cross exactly in the center of the southwest side of the painting. Was Mondrian moving toward crystalline symmetry?

But Butor points out that the vertical line is somewhat thinner than the horizontal one. A minimal asymmetry animates this painting. Mondrian flirts with crystals in order to bring out the most superficial tensions; the most spiritual ones, he says. For the eccentricity of the diagonals carves up the painting into surfaces of unequal value: the bottom left quadrant contracts, whereas its counterpart on the upper right expands. A play of tensions runs throughout the painting, and the two black lines are subjected to the unbalancing of the surfaces. So much so that according to Butor the painting can be seen as a sort of skylight opened onto a miniature Dutch landscape. The vertical reflection of the moon on the water cuts through the horizon of that flat country. But it is clearly the surface of the painting that makes this landscape resonate. The painting becomes a polder where the earth gives itself over to the undulations of the sea and quivers like a kite. Mondrian's quasi-crystal frees the power of the flattest land as it gives it over to inflection.

We believe that our classification of images is the visual counterpart of Simondon's statements. On the one hand, there are our three primary images, inflection, vector, and frame, that confer visibility on the potential field, polarization, and crystal, respectively. On the other, there are the intermediate categories, fluctuation, vector of concavity, and the modern quasi-frame, that confer visibility on Simondon's three other categories: molecular alea, germ of crystallization, and precrystalline forms of individuation. What is interesting in this process of making visible is that it allows us to widen the domain of our aesthetic classification of images to any field of individuation, be it biological, social, psychological, or other.

For we conceive of human beings as fluctuating between the extreme images that we have categorized as fluctuation and frame, in a sort of back-and-forth where the simple positions—one, two, and three—mark the formal stages in an overall process of individuation. There would thus be a first movement, that of fluctuation toward crystals, where being would be stored in intermediary images as a tendency at most. Then, following a passage through a frame, there would be a second movement: a turning back where tendency would become vector, and fluctuation inflection. Such is the pendulum motion of being that we wish to describe.

The originating point of oscillation is prior to inflection, in the domain of aleatory, though already qualified, configurations. These can be found in the fractal figures of Mandelbrot as well as in the pictorial experiences of Pollock or in the fluctuations of the wind on the surface of the water in Hokusai's drawings. Meanwhile, on the other side of fluctuation, inflection traces its concavities and convexities that in turn send off their vectors of curvature. Fluctuation becomes tendency, which is always multiple. And as it has no point of application, it will manifest itself through the strange qualities of evasion and nonadherence. For though tendency may become amplified on its own, it will not become a real vector as long as it hasn't passed through a frame. This passage can occur in one of two ways:

- Either the frame is a fully tertiary image and its aim is to allow no play. All fluctuations or tendencies are then captured by a crystal that creates a definitive polarity on the surface of the potential field. In this case, the structure drains off all possible becomings of the field.
- Or the frame isn't really a tertiary image. It is then a quasi-crystal that allows for a reverse movement that takes us through genuinely secondary and primary images.

"Genuinely secondary" refers to images that are properly vectorial; i.e., neither thrust nor escape, but will or capture. They refer to a force in its obstinate sense, where any departure is only a way of charging back again with increased determination; it is a consequence of the passage through the stability of the frame. Here we recognize a number of images: the gravitational vector, crystalline polarity, but also a monument profiled against the horizon, or the expression of a face in a portrait.

"Genuinely primary" then refers to those smooth and polished images that emerge after a time from genuinely secondary ones, after they have exhausted all reactions from the medium and act in such a way as to give rise only to virtualities of action and reaction. Action and reaction then no longer form an antagonism but compose a play of possibilities. Resistance gives way to transistance. Force is no longer measured in terms of action or determination, but in terms of its potential for variable application. The abstract sign of this genuine primariness is of course inflection: a singularity open to the play of vectors in the passage from one gravity to another—toward lightness. And the concrete images of primariness can be found in the rounded shape of a pebble, in the whiteness of a bone unearthed, in the polished handle of a tool, or in the incurvation of the worn steps of a staircase made of stone. It is the luminosity of jade as opposed to the brilliance of crystal. It is like the very smooth quality of someone who's been around; it's what an old person's smile can sometimes be.

The roundedness of primary images then constitutes a smooth background upon which new fractalizations are incised. They are differential fluctuations of another kind: a new age of individuation is born. The loose meshing of the quasi-crystal allows the preindividualized to emerge in the form of a new roughness. Whether it be made of granite or of velvet, this roughness is an image that throws everything into question. Either fluctuation spreads to the roundedness and carries inflection toward absolute chance; or, conversely, each fluctuation becomes the space of vectors of concavity and of new tendencies. At the endpoint of the return to primariness, the overflowing toward fractalization appears as a symmetrical alternative to the one we had noted at the extremity of crystal. Either the movement of fractalization goes too far and we fall into aleatory death, or else a spin-about allows us to turn back and find tendency once again.

There are therefore two ways of dying or of being

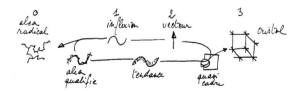

ejected from the great oscillation of life. For at the two extremities of the back-and-forth of images, we always find these two sorts of moves in the circus of life: On the side of crystal, you have to be able to jump through the frame, the hoop, or the trapeze, then go into a spiral and land as a vector or the affirmation of a will. On the side of inflection, the act is quite different. The acrobat becomes a clown. The flea tamer calls upon its roundedness an alea that it senses as an itch. Then the clown, white, smooth, and polished, must remove itself from the chancy contortions of a Titus who is constantly running great dangers.

These are then the two very peculiar acts at the extreme ends of inflection and crystal where, each time, the recovery calls for a backing up. Alea and crystal are the boundaries of life, the maximum oscillation between the two figures of death. Inflection and vector are the only simple positions of life, but as such they are transitory. For we usually only deal with intermediary images that are never polished and are always fractal, just as they are never voluntary and are always indecisive. And as long as there is life, there is neither crystal nor alea, but an oscillation between the two. With the first motion of the pendulum, we remain chance without ever really acceding to quality, or else we follow tendencies that don't have the determination of a vector. But conversely, with the return of the pendulum, we hold onto the frame instead of recovering elegantly after jumping through the crystal. We remain stubborn resistance instead of acceding to the transistance of inflection.

One back-and-forth, one complete oscillation, is a period of individuation. If we take crystallization to be the first material individuation, other individuations must be seen as inserting themselves into this process: prebiotic, then biological ones, social ones, and finally psychological ones. Each of these further individuations would be a double detour or a delay between stochastic and crystalline death. For each additional oscillation would seek the frame of the quasi-crystal that would allow it to turn back rather than to be trapped by the crystal. Thus each endpoint of the oscillation would set up mechanisms of anticipation-conjuration that would tell us where to go too far, either toward chance or toward crystal, such that each back-and-forth would constitute an instance of a more general pattern of evolution. The simplest way of thinking about it is that oscillations follow one another and lie upon one another like the folds of a cloth. And it is very likely that the stages of life articulated by each oscillation also constantly cross over into one another, like so many sheets of dough that are being kneaded together by a baker.

Let us take the example of the frames of individuation that were categorized by structuralism. The validity of this method has been greatly contested and is even scoffed at today. And yet, while we do not wish to return to the past, we think it might be interesting to reevaluate a number of images that have been neglected by structuralism, both from a conceptual as well as from an aesthetic perspective. The most interesting aspect of structuralist theories as a whole is that they allow us to think of individuation as a passage through the frame of tertiary images, starting with the gift. But unfortunately, the structuralists themselves got tangled up in the web of structure and precipitated their thinking toward crystalline death. As Aesop said: "Structure is the best and the worst of things."

From very early on, the structuralists did in fact only pay attention to crystalline forms. But if we go back to the inaugural text, *The Elementary Structures of Kinship*, it becomes clear that the structural apparatus set forth by Lévi-Strauss only makes sense in relation to the continuum of nature. Social structures are built upon the biological phylum and they construct the frames that will isolate the human species from a genocidal base. This biological phylum appears as a genuinely primary image. Biological individuation unfolds a surface on which the sexual sphere acquires the value of a singularity: it is a relief that traces a zone of determination; it is a passage or a peak after which the parting of the waters becomes equivocal. Nature seems to have planned everything except the choice of a mate. A fractalization of the biological group follows from this. Chance is introduced into the civility of nature and gives rise to a whole range of affective tendencies. It is the passage through the frames of exchange that will turn these tendencies into forms of desire. A new surface then covers the first: it is the field of emotions.

One would have to go back to the structuralist texts and point out in each case the continua upon which the structures are built: the sexual continuum, the affective continuum, the sound continuum, the action continuum, etc. These represent a whole range of primary images that constitute as many spheres of individuation with respect to the frames of the structure. One would then have to distinguish those structures that operate like crystals and block the individuation of the potential field from those that allow, as do quasi-crystals, the free play of various strategies to unfold: therein lies the entire question of the existence of genuinely dualistic mechanisms in *Structural Anthropology*.

In fact, Lévi-Strauss never stopped raising the question of false symmetries and loose structures that bring about inequality in the context of exchange. For structures can then be thought of as absolutely abstract forms, capable of framing any concrete continuum.

There could thus be a social framing of the sexual continuum, as in matrimonial exchange; a sound framing of the action continuum, as in work rhythms, etc. Abstract structures could then be classified by evaluating their permeability with respect to a number of concrete continua. One simple frame could structure several continua, but, conversely, one continuum could become individuated through different structures. Thus the layers formed by the successive oscillations of life become susceptible to a deep kneading process that would mix together, as it were, the different phases of life: language and crystallization, hominization and photonic quanta. Life works itself out through a kneading process that is close to that of thought itself.[6]

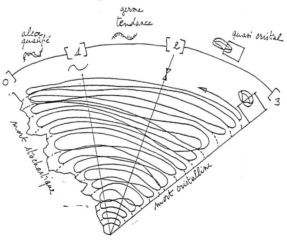

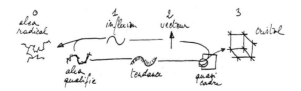

ten Body and Soul

To have a body is neither simpler nor more complicated than to have a mind. For body and mind are made of the same thing, of the only thing that is, which is neither spiritual nor corporeal, and which, like others, we will call substance.

This substance is a priori nothing other than a fact of curvature. As such, its principal activity is to produce concavity and convexity in an inverted mode.

To keep matters simple, let us consider this substance a kind of surface that has one curvature or another. This surface has a front side and a back side, the one being concave when the other is convex. Even more than a surface, substance is an interface, a converter of signs of concavity.

Among other things, this means that the radii of curvature of the surface converge on the concave side and diverge on the convex side. In any given zone, where the sign and the value of the curve remain relatively stable, it is possible to determine a center of curvature where the cluster of radii of curvature converge.

Let us call "souls" the sites of convergence on one of the sides, and "bodies" the sites of convergence on the other. These sides will then be called respectively thought and extension.

Body and soul are thus constructed in the same manner, at the intersection of a cluster of radii of curvature. Both are then simply effects of convergence that are constituted in space, on either side of the surface of the world that envelops them. It follows that the body is no less ideal than the mind, despite the claims of those who would like to see it as something material or tangible.

The ideal case would of course be that of a zone of constant curvature, the arc of a circle or a spherical dome. In this case, the radii converge toward one single

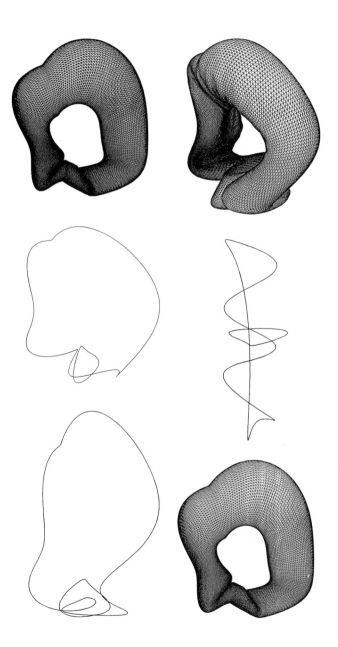

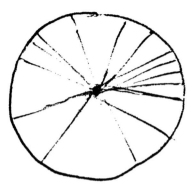

point, which is the center that "explains" the circle or the sphere.

It would seem then that the world was designed by an architect who planted his compasses from soul to body, following the succession of inversions of curvature. But let us make no mistake; it is the curvature of the world that in turn designs the soul of the architect and so on, indefinitely, or at least very far. The world is not the curve that links the different circles that the architect would have drawn from center to center; on the contrary, bodies and souls are events of convergence that are produced in space on either side of substance.

The fortuitous nature of bodies and souls appears more clearly if one examines the concrete universe of surfaces with undetermined curvature. Here, the radii no longer really converge and there is no visible center where the architect might have planted his compasses. Each part of the surface, no matter how small, only constitutes one site of variation of the center of curvature;

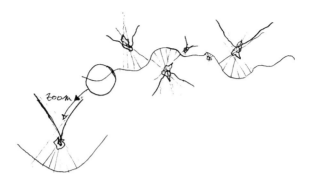

at best, this site of convergences becomes invaginated, but in most cases, it is the site of an accident, a loop or a backup point among branches that go off to infinity. Here and there haloes are formed, the line of variation of the center of curvature turns back on itself and oscillates, at least for a while; in these recesses, an embryo of body and soul is formed. We are here reducing this dark zone to the clarity of a point, but one must see that bodies and souls do not form a seedbed of isolated points that scintillate in space on either side of the world; they are themselves zones of variation that are often more complex than the world. We did suspect that to reduce substance to a surface world was but a first approximation; we now see that to speak of that substance presupposes at the very least that one confront a principle of generation of surfaces, of complex stratification of events of concavity and convexity.

But this should not prevent us from examining classical figures very closely. A mathematician of the old school would have lots to tell us about the family of cycloids. But we shall now examine a line with constant curves, such as the outside contour of a rosette, a daisy, or an ideal pumpkin. Each of the circular arcs has its own well-defined center of curvature; it can be said that they have a soul, or, just as easily, that they form a body. But these small arcs are inscribed within a large circle that envelops them and that itself has a center. Better yet, the center of the large enveloping circle is also the center of the circle that links the centers of the small arcs. We are thus dealing with a composite soul or body, with a soul that explains other souls, or with bodies that imply other bodies.

In this way we can see more clearly what it means to have a body or to have a soul, and mainly what the subject of this "to have" might be. For only substance projects this cluster that converges toward a soul or a body; only it is subjectile. But only the radii of a limited zone can converge and, even so, only more or less well. The subjectile thus subdivides into "subject" zones of which it will be said that they have this body or that soul.

The rosette showed us that the texture of substance is the inclusion of envelopes that fold into one another, small circles into large ones. We will then certainly not acquire the soul or the body that we are at such pains to secure by better enclosing our subject zones; we must rather delve down into texture or go back up into envelopes by grafting ourselves onto the world that sur-rounds us and by opening this world within us. We have

to learn to modulate our zones: to dance to recover a
body in the envelope of the tribe, or to fade away to
acquire a soul within the texture of thought.

Here several attitudes are possible. According to the
state of curvature one believes the world to be in, one
can see it as a soul of souls, a plane of souls, or a surface
of souls. The world is thus either a unique soul that
curves about us to form a sphere; or it is a plane of souls
projected toward infinity; or it is forever thrown off by a
substance that forms a plane of immanence. Leibniz's
sphere of infinite radii and Spinoza's plane that makes of
parallelism a case of absolute nonconvergence are cases
of categorical rejections of the body of bodies and the
soul of souls. And, most likely, the unspecified curvature
that always varies is not a soul of souls either, but the
soul of a few souls, or a soul inasmuch as there is a body.

But so far we are pretending that the body and the
soul are similar. And it is true that they have to do with
the same conceptual construct that is found at the intersection of radii perpendicular to the world. One reality,
substance, suffices, and the perspective on concavity
becomes arbitrary; however, once these points of view
are fixed, they preclude each other. Sufficient reason and
the principle of absolute contradiction. It is always possible to call body what others call mind, but nonetheless
these landscapes are different and are not interchangeable. For the concavities of the soul form the convexities
of the body. And as there are no indications that the curvatures of the world are symmetrical, one side is not

equivalent to the other. Analogy of construct goes hand in hand with radical difference. Though they are both ideal, bodies and souls are nonetheless in absolute phasal opposition. Worse yet, what is explicit for one will be implicit for the other. It will in fact be quite an art to distinguish which side is the most explicit according to the circumstances or affects. Shall I go to my analyst or my neurologist? For substance is no doubt psychosomatic, but, precisely, its effects will be better explained sometimes on its somatic side, sometimes on its psychical side. Unless we are very sick or very much alive from inhabiting a substance whose curvature constantly reverses itself, there is no concavity, no matter how slight, that does not harbor a convexity, and vice versa; there is no body without an intercalated soul, nor a soul without a body that is inserted into it.

Without even envisaging such cases, we will have to closely examine a few singular points of substance. For the essence of curvature is that it can vary continually, provoking disruptions at the points that are the centers of curvature. Let us first examine the simplest case: that of two inverted semicircles that are nonetheless related. As in the Tao figure of yin and yang, we can see a point of convergence precisely at the center of each semicircle. We will say that these points designate respectively the body and the soul of this element of substance.

Now let us think of this in a progressive manner, as if we were slowly traveling along the curvature, linking to each momentary position the center of curvature of our movement. As long as we remain on the first circle, we only point to the first center; we will do the same with the second center when we move onto the second circle; but in the interval, what do we do? What happens at the point of junction that marks the inflection of our movement? How do we jump from one point to anoth-

er? How do we get from the body to the soul? The
Chinese resolved this geometrical problem by inscribing
the figure in a circle whose center was precisely the
point of inflection. Was this their way of resolving the
problem of the unity between the body and the soul, by
invoking a point of harmony that was the empty center
of the universe?

Leibniz, for his part, seems to refer to baroque
inflection with its characteristic slippage. Between the
two inverse swirls, each converging toward its center of
curvature, a distended inflection ensures the continuity
between these inverse curvatures that are less and less
pronounced as they reach the limit case of the straight
line: the tangent merges with the curve that it crosses at
the point of inflection. At this singular point, the center
of curvature escapes to the infinity of the soul, and God
sends it back to us on the other side, from an infinity of
the body.

For such is the ambiguous nature of baroque inflection, that singular point of substance that is explained by
a body as well as by a soul; it is the only point of which it
will be said that it has a body and a soul, while at the
same time it is a place of rupture of the site of bodies as

of souls. Bodies and souls in tatters, on either side of substance. A radical discontinuity that is resolved only through a passage to infinity.

But we must also consider another singular configuration of substance: a second nature of inflection. For inflection is not a figure in itself; it is a family of configurations; it is in fact a double series. Our first baroque inflection established a continuity of substance between an infinity of the body and an infinity of the soul, a substantial continuity between the values of curvature that reverse signs as they pass through infinity. But instead of reversing signs, why not simply pass through a zero of curvature and find a configuration of substance that ensures the continuous passage from convexity to concavity, a point that turns on itself, where the circumference is nowhere other than at its center?

This second inflection is in fact not necessarily different from the first. In order to explain its functioning, one could draw a double inverted spiral of which one branch would spin faster and faster, until it turns on itself with a radius of curvature that is reduced to nothing and can then reverse signs and give birth to a second branch, whose curvature will become increasingly diminished: a sort of cosmic, swirling embryo. But for those with an eye for differential geometry, such a demonstrative figure is unnecessary; a simple inversion of curvature suffices, so long as it passes through a point of annulment or of self-vertigo [*vertige sur soi*].

inflexion simple   ligne des centres de courbure   inflexion maniériste

inflexion
seconde

lieu des
centres de courboures

inflexion
rococo

For the true distinction between these two inflections is of an energetic order. The first inflection is inertial; its rectification minimizes the swerves of a subject submitted to centrifugal force. The second, on the other hand, is vibrative and calls upon a specific type of energy: a rotation on itself that is similar to the spin of particles in modern physics. While the first inflection is a point of release of substance, the second designates zones of intensity where high elementary energies come together. Leibniz may have been right when he said that atoms were not like grains of sand but like folds on a sheet of slate.

And moreover, by ensuring a continuity between concavity and convexity, the second inflection inscribes the sites of the body and the soul on one same surface that now crosses substance at its point. So far, we understood how the body and the soul explain the respective zones of the world that implies them. We can now locate points of complication, singularities where substance

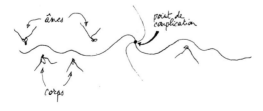

âmes

point de
complication

corps

complicates the body and the soul in the world, yet without having to resort to a passage through infinity.

It must of course be said that these are but a cluster of disparate thoughts that we are trying to bring together. We have used the word "body" to designate that which "embodies" within the unnamable world of our daily perceptions. This concept of body is nothing other than an abstract site of convergence that concerns a particular zone of substance, and this, moreover, only on the side we are used to calling material, in the same way as we call soul, or thought, the sites of convergence on the other side. As for substance, it is much closer to what we usually call our body, which is to say that mix of dreams and intoxications, of sufferings and hallucinations, that are as intermingled as are the two sides of a sheet of paper. For we can rest assured that substance accomplishes fully well the task of combining extension and thought, the interface of the psyche and the soma, to the point where it is in fact quite unbearable. We can only emerge from this confusion through the complication of a body and soul, and the inscription of these two abstract events on a surface that fastens down substance.

Traditionally, we call body that part of substance that is caught in the sack of our skin. Certain things such as mirrors, or language, have us believing that it is indeed a coherent whole, something like a ball closed around a center. We would in fact love to be closed in on ourselves, to cut ourselves away from substance and form a circuit with our own little perceptions and affects. But we are all already caught in substance, that complex fact of concavities and convexities. As it is, what we take to be our body is in the first place a toric envelope. Our flesh coils about the conduits through which the outside traverses us. Our toric destiny would have it that the orifices of all our conduits are but illusory closures. With our sex organs in our mouths, our body envelops a new concavity that passes through us. The torus goes back to the torus; forever. And thank God for that, for if we keep pretending to be sacks, we might gain a body, but we will certainly lose our souls. Because the torus, like a flesh chamber, allows for two sites of convergence: a line runs inside the tire and is the site of the centers of each of its sections, but this does not prevent the gut from curving about the hub. If our body is a torus, we can then have a body and a soul. Let us even say that we can't escape the soul. We are in fact very similar to those primary inflections that envelop on both sides a body and a soul. But will we be able to find the secondary inflection that complicates body and soul within substance?

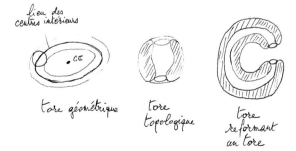

lieu des
centres intérieurs

. CE

tore géométrique

tore
topologique

tore
reformant
un tore

eleven **Réflexion**

A tubular chair in nickel-plated aluminum in the tradition of Marcel Breuer. Both tubes are shaped like an inflection, but in one it is more pronounced than in the other. They are linked by elastic ties and generate a pleated surface. Both are soldered onto a metallic base that mirrors the image of the chair. The tubes are one meter apart. The surface that is near the more taut inflection is not habitable and is only used to lay down clothes, but it is possible to sit on the other part of the pleat. This chair could be used in a fitting room.

The tubular chair is reflected in its metallic base, and, as the two tubes are at right angles to the reflective plane, the reflected image is inscribed in the continuity of the object. The pleat is continued on a symmetrical surface that offers an alternate perception. From a purely optical point of view, the continuity of the object and its reflection form a single image, and the qualities of the double surface will be considered independently of the existence of each of the two sides. From a purely sensorimotor point of view, however, truth and error will be distributed on either side of the reflective plane according to our tactile control. In this second view, our body reassures itself as it finds a resistance with respect to which it senses its own reactive powers.

What we take to be our vision is permeated by touch. But then our touch is but one part of the sensorimotor apparatus thanks to which we grasp things such as objects: by maximizing our actions and reactions. In fact, we rather mistrust those optical images that escape us and whose effects are beyond our reach. As if we were unable to see, we insist on placing the truth at the extremities of our limbs; but what is wrong with a vision that attaches itself to untouchable objects? In these audiovisual times, we may not live up to our eyes, and may entirely miss the optical experience that Bergson

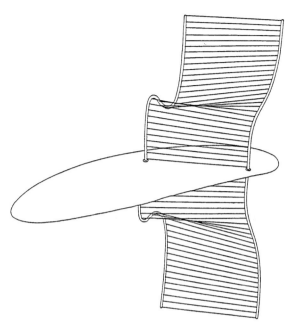

took as being at the origin of the soul in primitive ways of thinking.[7]

For our reflection in a mirror would seem to invite us to remove the top layer of our skin from our bodies. "There is a body that is removable from the one we touch, a body without an inside, without gravity." That optical body bears our singularity independently of our existence, since we see it where we aren't, and yet nothing resembles us more. This possibility of our acceding to quality independently of our presence was, for Bergson, the basis of our belief that the soul survives us after our death.

But the mirror has to do with life. "The other side of the mirror" does not take us back to a world that is symmetrical to that of the living, where we find once again the closed images of identity. For in fact we are already on the other side, and the most important thing is to know how to come back: through the glass and crystalline identities. As long as the side we see in the mirror is the only one in question, our unified image puts the veil of singularity in the bag of identity.

But it is not a question of going behind the mirror either; we must rather push images toward the side of things themselves in order to rediscover their quality. As we extend our hand toward our image, we break the closure of our reflection, and the optical and the tactile body become a continuity that forms one single surface of variable curvature. Touch itself is then freed from our sensorimotor apparatus and lets the feel of the texture of things enter into the optical image. As it faces two images that are oriented in an inverse manner, our eye, in a state of weightlessness, is directed toward intrinsic singularities, and our tactile sensations resonate with the optical surface that has dissolved objects as it detaches them from their existence. It is as if life didn't belong to existence, for the latter is never anything other than sensorimotor. Bergson may have been right to declare death to death and thus to speak of a life without existence. Of the soul perhaps.

twelve **Mémoire**

A living room in an apartment that overlooks Lac Léman in Montreux. The coffee table is inserted into a bookcase whose variable-curvature surface runs along the wall. The glass plate of the table allows us to see two characteristic shapes of the local landscape: a small island combined with a mountainside.

In the Montreux apartment, the furniture reproduces the landscape, not as a reflection but as a miniature. There is no mirror; only a window that opens onto the lake and sets up the frame of the laws of perspective. Through the window, the surface of the table is a model that echoes the landscape. The mountain becomes a sculpture in the round; what is big becomes small. It is strange that this most obvious aspect of perspective is often ignored. For beyond relativizing the point of view, perspective is that art that allows us to hold a mountain between our fingers. It is a strange optic that threatens purely mechanical relations: the big can be contained in the small, the outside in the inside. Perspective proposes a logic of sacks rather than one of boxes: A contains B, which doesn't prevent B from being able to contain A. The window frames the landscape as much as the landscape encompasses the frame. The model is an image that makes this inside-outside visible as it flees along the lines of a world in perspective and obliges us to place ourselves outside ourselves. Our entire subjectivity lies in the perspective of a miniaturized world. Our perception is the image of the world in our brain. As long as we think of images in the mode of representation, we are caught in the sack of a logic that reduces the world to the cerebral images that we form of it, whereas in fact the brain is itself but a part of the images of the world. All we need to do is to leave images where we see them, which is to say in things themselves. We have gotten into the habit of classifying images in our inside while

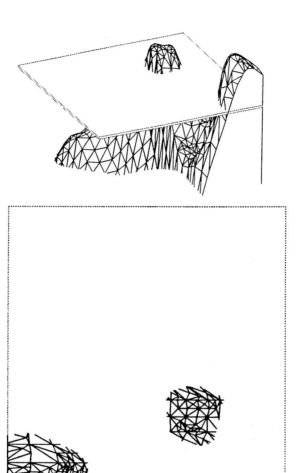

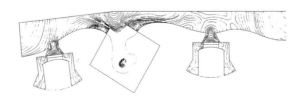

leaving things outside of ourselves. That is because things act upon us without our noticing them, whereas we see images in our dreams that act upon us very little. On one hand, then, we place outside the "real" things that act upon us without our necessarily forming an image of them, while on the other hand, we keep inside those perceptual images that appear to us all the more clearly as their action upon us is somehow suspended.

But our perception does not consist in that luminosity of inactive images within the obscurity of active things. On the contrary, the things that are present and that we don't perceive are images in the full light of day; they are absolutely translucid and they give back all that they receive as they continually interact with each other and with us. Invisible because they are transparent, these images have neither form nor duration; they simply trace surfaces of propagation. But in this full light, certain images are less transparent and create zones of opacity that do not give in the same way as they receive. Along with Bergson (especially chapter 1 of *Matter and Memory*), we will call "body" any zone that introduces an opacity in the transmission of interactions. Rather than a space of densification, the body then appears as a deficit within universal communication, as a loss of contact that produces indetermination within luminous transmission.

There is thus body in nature wherever there is an indetermination with respect to a milieu; wherever something that is localized escapes global conditions. Thus there are bodies in rivers where unpredictable whirlpools form, but inversely, our limbs are out-of-body as long as they remain transparent with respect to certain physical phenomena. We don't perceive hertz waves because our behavior has no impact on their propagation. That is what allows Bergson to say that we perceive things that are outside of ourselves. Our perceptions do indeed take place within our body, but the corporeality of our body is always only partial. The body in which perception takes place generally remains transparent to the interactions for which it is nothing more than a surface of propagation. Here and there a few images are retained, but fundamentally our perception is formed by the out-of-body images that only pass through our limbs. At this degree zero, our perception is thus certainly not a miniature, and our body, far from being a screen of representation, simply offers a surface of propagation that prolongs the very nature of things.

But the basis of out-of-body images is not perception itself. Bergson said that we perceive according to our actions upon things. What then are our actions? In what way can we act upon the fabric of interactions?

The first answer is simple but negative: we are able to wait. The body introduces an interval between a solicitation and a reaction. Our body is that delay that is available to us before we react, during which time images are drawn—images that seem to us to be less than things, precisely because they have no direct effect on us. But how is it that we can wait? Bergson's real answer is that we act in such a way that our reactions are not only determined by our present state of being, but also by our previous ones. For Bergson, action is a contraction of the past in the present of our reactions. Thus color perception is in itself an action, because in a yellow or blue color, we contract a great number of vibrations to their corresponding frequency. A simple quality gathers onto itself a series of instantaneous states. We can then not, a fortiori, account for any of our actions without placing ourselves in a duration that comprises a multiplicity of elementary gestures. "I am walking" contracts the succession of my steps. One must also add that for

Bergson, what is elementary is not in any way an objective given; it is only the result of a loosening of a contraction. A single element is but a release of the present; it is never definitive, for otherwise it would rejoin the out-of-body of the instantaneous interaction of images.

As it is a contraction, perception places us immediately within memory, where the present is determined by the past. For memory has two aspects: inscription on one hand, and contraction on the other. But first and foremost, memory is a faculty of the body, and all of Bergsonian philosophy has but one object: memory as the incapacity of the body. As inscription, memory is immediate, and it fully preserves the past in its singularity. Nothing is more opposed to the positivity of memory than an engrammic conception of it: inscription, at first glance, is full and whole because memory as a "faculty" is absolutely different from those grooves that are progressively burrowed, erasing the singularity of each of its impressions.

The lesson that is learned by heart is no longer but a reflex, while the lessons of the heart draw our attention to the singularity of each of our recollections when the text was present but not yet known. Between the engram and the groove, the indetermination of the body fades away. Only the process of learning is a faculty, while the conditioning of our responses to the solicitations of the milieu closes onto themselves the automatisms of the out-of-body of interactions rather than opening up a zone of indetermination.

In fact it would seem that the body carries an automaton as its shadow. The indetermination of interactions presupposes the setting up of automatisms through which our reactions escape more and more from the milieu. That is why we drag along a solid body, though corporeality in itself is an emptying out. That is what Bergson meant by false movement. Mechanics make us think that the body is like a mobile whose parts are all determined with respect to one another, which is why we also think that movement is reducible to trajectory alone. On the contrary, Bergson tells us, real movement lies in the qualitative changes of the milieu in which the mobile moves about. As its position changes, the relations among the mobile, its parts, and the milieu also change, endowing the whole with a new quality. Sweetened water is of a different nature than water that contains sugar.

But the mobile image can be criticized on another level as well. The billiard ball appears as a solid body and the play between the parts is regulated once and for all. The full body of the mobile is thus a zone of automatism where the trajectory of the object is entirely determined by the impact on the peripheral parts. The solidarity between the parts thus expresses the very opposite of an indetermination of interactions within a milieu. And in particular, the movement of the center of the billiard ball is entirely determined by the events that transpire at a distance that is set once and for all: the radius of the sphere. Yet it is this rigid circumference that interests Bergson, because for one, it draws the limit that allows us to separate the fate of the mobile and the immobile; that is what prevents us from grasping the qualitative changes of the whole. We therefore reduce the duration of the whole to the space covered by the mobile alone. But mainly, this limit circumscribes the present of the mobile whose trajectory is entirely determined by its circumference, which is given once and for all. This is then the very opposite of memory, which is that faculty of the body that makes of the past the horizon of a variable present. The body is therefore always to be made, as it constantly modulates its limit in time and space.

For memory now appears in its dual aspect: as inscription, it is immediate and total; as engram, it sets up the automatisms of a mineralized body; but as contraction, memory has the capacity of folding the surface of universal inscription as it forms the overfold of variable engrams. In each instance, memory carries different modalities of the present.[8] As inscription, it locates the moment in an eternal return. As engram, it closes the present onto itself by setting equivalences between solicitations and reactions. But finally, as contraction, it introduces a deficit in the present of equivalences. Sometimes, reactions can be prior to solicitations and can sometimes even become part of the out-of-body of simple transmission. The circumference widens: the present overflows onto both the past and the future. It is the moment of investment or of contraction of solicitations with respect to reactions that are progressively more distant and uncertain, for engrams do not let themselves be folded without introducing a certain amount of give in the overlay of their composition. At other times, however, reactions exhaust solicitations. The entire past becomes concentrated in the present of an excessive reaction that can reach the point of threatening the reproduction of the automatisms themselves.

It would then seem that our body lies in that intermediary zone between the out-of-body of radical interactions and the mineralized body of our automatisms. Or rather, like a magnetic field, our body would encroach upon both of these two zones. We would then win over the out-of-body inasmuch as we dispose of a certain amount of time before reacting to solicitations; and we would win over the mineralized body to the extent that we introduce caesuras within our automatisms. All this leads to a greater modulation of the present, as it allows us to cover all the different states of tension that are available to us.

We have already seen that our perception was founded on the out-of-body of interactions to which our limbs are also submitted; but that did not really concern perception itself, which is that status of images with respect to which we dispose of a margin of indetermination. We now see that our perception takes place as there is an increase in the field of images between the out-of-body of interactions and the mineralized body of our automatisms. That is why, once again, Bergson could say that we perceive outside of ourselves: that is to say outside of our solid bodies and of the zones of our automatisms. Our perception is that body of images whose variable horizon expresses our potential for action.

In this sense perception consists of two parts that could be called frontal and longitudinal. The frontality of perceived images would result from their action being suspended with respect to us; from the break between their solicitation and our reaction—an interval between our automatisms. The second part would then be longitudinal as we constantly expose ourselves to out-of-body images in order to always redefine the present of our perception or the variable horizon of our contractile body. According to the frontal component, we see clear articulations drawn between the objects that solicit the reactions of our solid body; while longitudinally, each of these images continually interacts with the others and with us, as in a test of resonance. For we must produce the tone of our present in order to adjust the horizon of our contractile body and find the right pitch. Unlike the great frontal articulations, our longitudinal perception constantly folds and rubs the fabric of images against itself, thus allowing the texture of things to emerge.

That is why classicism was troubled by perspectivism. It had certainly become possible to construct the articulation of forms in space by projecting them upon the frontal plane of the painting. But that entailed some doubt as to their relative size. Longitudinally, the beams of the visual pyramid confused the large and the small. Hence, in the margins of representational scenes, the theme of the dwarf would become so important. Indeed, this enigmatic character raises the question of perspective with respect to frontal images. Is it a distant view of an adult or a close-up of a child? We find a very relative answer to this question in the space of relations between the figures in *Las Meninas*, for example. But certain painters raised this same question without the help of this sort of space. They tried to veil the articulations of the frontal plane and painted the dwarf alone, outside of any architectural reference. They took the risk of confusing proximity and distance, youth and old age. The only possible solution was to rely on the texture of the skin: the dwarf's skin was not the same as the adult's or the child's, and some Spanish artists excelled at reproducing this texture against the backdrop of curtains. Instead of frontal articulations we then have the longitudinal folds of textures: the dermis of the dwarf against a velvety fabric.

Painting would thus once again play upon the clash of man against the plane of orthogonality to movement. The flattening out of the crucifixion on the two axes of frontal coordinates, then the radial organization of that plane around the point of view: that point of impact of subjectivity on the frontal plane would have been a first moment in the history of painting; our perception was then constituted around the stoppage of movement, or the break in our automatisms. And that first moment would be followed by this second one: the transformation of the frontal plane into a longitudinal surface. Once projected upon the frontal plane, the painting had to be made to resonate, to allow the texture of images to emerge, to experience the tone of a variable present. This was the real significance of the impressionist break: to focus exclusively on the texture of corporealities within the play of light. This movement would of course be furthered by Michaux, Pollock, or Zao-Wou-Ki.

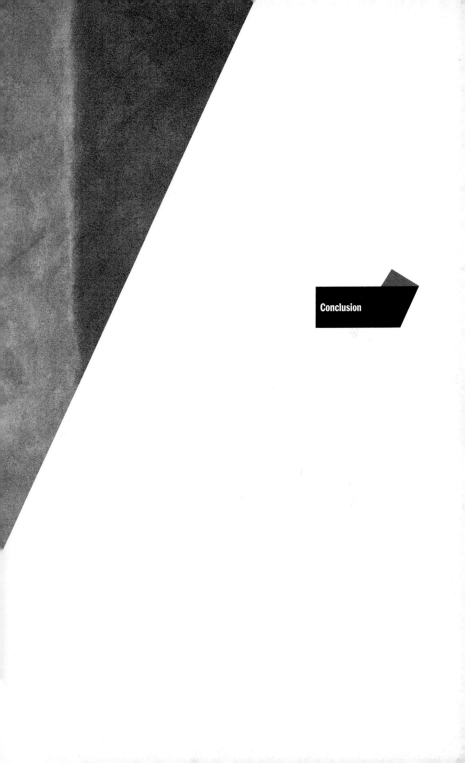

Conclusion

Our times are such that we seek the outside on the inside, geography in furniture, but also images in things themselves. That is true of territories, where the gridding of the politics of planning seems to have exhausted all the potentialities of sites. The particularities of the relief itself presents obstacles that might at best be restored in the name of local particularism. For machines, in any case, will flatten the site, so that the respect of its contour becomes a sort of reconstruction. This is also true in the case of cinema, where characters are flattened as the same stories are told over and over again and become interchangeable. Strong singularities erode and give way to softened fluctuations. Like the last fits of an encephalogram before it goes flat?

Unless fluctuation is changing the nature of singularity. People in previous times had an aristocratic manner of domination; they were extremities, as it were. Even the lowliest excelled in their own way, while today we only see inconsistency: people without singularity, prepared to maximize anything at all. But as personalities dissolve into fluctuations, the singular moves away from the extremities toward the in-between of inflection. The surface of variable curvature of man-as-skin resonates with the fluctuations in tone of an amortized Earth. The work of art is no longer of nature but *de naturanda*. Geography may be a gift; it may be our only fortune. Variation in curvature, which is nonoptimizable, is where the most is not worth more than the least, but is worth something in the inflected passage from the more to the less. The modern continuum raises the following question: are we dealing with the inconsistency of fluctuation or with the transistance of inflection?

And this question is well worth a monument. A modern monument, no longer historical, but geographical, for a memory that is more contractile than engrammic. Not necessarily large, and maybe even small: just an image. Thus we move from the imposing monument to the transistant monument. The sacrificial monument, column or obelisk, determined the reading of a site. And it was monumental; it immobilized the vector and designated eminences. The modern monument, on the other hand, ensures the transistance from one reading to another. The ground itself becomes a sculpture: a variable curvature outside of any vector. Territorial politics must now go through a series of readings, in the same way as the richness of a population is measured by the breadth of its gene pool. It is an art of the passage from one reading to another for our audiovisual times. Fortunately, cinema has no more stories to tell, which means that it can find images in things. A monument will be able to stand on film when a productive cinema will accede to the primary image: a new geographical possibility, our response to the Earth. Such was the promise of Godard's short film on Lausanne.

Notes

1. "Sloped city, crest city, perched city, valley city": these four urban figures form a typology borrowed from a local historian, Charles Biermann.

2. Le Corbusier also reduced modern architecture to five fundamental elements: the flat roof, stilts, elongated windows, the free facade, and the free plan.

3. Decried as the symbol of Communist architecture, the flat roof often raises, from the point of view of construction, as many problems as it solves, nor is it the sign of the advent of a Communist society.

4. Nietzsche wrote: "Man, that disease of the skin of the earth."

5. On the evolution of the juridical system, see the work of François Ewald. He argues that the framework of liberal law only supplies a general structure of juridical principles that are articulated by the tensions of the social fabric that in turn stabilize norms.

6. See Gilles Deleuze, *Cinema 2: The Time Image*, trans. Hugh Tomlinson and Robert Galeta (Minneapolis: University of Minnesota Press, 1989).

7. On the optical origin of the soul, see Henri Bergson, *The Two Sources of Morality and Religion*, chapter two.

8. In Stoicism everything exists in the present, even the past.

Cover image by Jacques Hampe. Objectiles photos by Patrick Renaud and Marie Combes. All other photos by Franz Graf. Handmade furniture by Bernard Cache with François Cache and Patrick Beauce. Machined furniture by Cambium. Software programmed by Jean-Louis Jammot at TOPCAD. Research made possible by the Centre Technique du Bois et d'Ameublement (Woodworking and Furniture Center) and the French Ministry of Research.